THE GOSPEL OF MARK

At the Table: A Devotional for Individuals and Households

THE GOSPEL OF MARK
At the Table: A Devotional for Individuals and Households

Cover by:
Emily Carpenter
Joy Everlasting Photography

 Indy-Ref Press. Independent Reformed Books.

Printed by Amazon Create Space services in Lexington, KY.
Available for purchase at www.amazon.com.

¹⁵ And as he reclined at table in his house, many tax collectors and sinners were reclining with Jesus and his disciples, for there were many who followed him.¹⁶ And the scribes of the Pharisees, when they saw that he was eating with sinners and tax collectors, said to his disciples, "Why does he eat with tax collectors and sinners?" ¹⁷ And when Jesus heard it, he said to them, "Those who are well have no need of a physician, but those who are sick. I came not to call the righteous, but sinners."

(Mark 2:15-17, ESV).

Read This First: An Introduction to this Book

The book in your hands could powerfully impact your personal devotional life this year as well as the spiritual life of your whole family. Or, to be completely honest, it could be a total flop. You may use it every week this year, or perhaps never even break in the binding of the cover.

It all depends on how you use it. As they say, "You get out of it what you put into it."

The reason that I put this resource together is that I have a passion to see the people in my own congregation encounter Jesus Christ in their homes and at their dinner tables. The subtitle, "At the Table" reflects my hope that the households in my church would in fact use it at the dinner table. Life gets pretty busy. Sometimes we need to stop, sit around the table with our loved ones, and reflect on what is important. Whether alone, or with a loved one, or at a messy, busy table surrounded by children. Again, it is all up to you.

Using this Book

This book provides a year's worth of devotions that are roughly based on our own worship services in the Reformed tradition. There are enough Scripture passages given in this book to take you through one year of devotions, as we work through the Gospel of Mark.

The opening prayer given for most weeks is a classic prayer from the *Book of Common Prayer,* that great, historical and spiritual guidebook of the Church of England, devised by our forefathers. I personally love this particular prayer, and use it all the time to ready my own heart. I would love it if you too would commit it to memory, and use it to open and begin your times in the Word. On other occasions you will open your devotional time with Psalm 95:1-7 which has been called the *Venite Exultamus Domino,* Latin for "Come let us exalt the Lord!"

After the opening prayer, you will find readings from the Gospel of Mark in either the ESV or NKJV versions. I hope that the very act of reading and thinking through these texts will be an enlightening experience for you and your family.

After that, you will find the Westminster Shorter Catechism. The word "catechism" is simply the Greek word that means "teaching" or "instruction" in the Bible. Since 1647, the Westminster Shorter Catechism has been the standard formula for teaching basic Christian doctrine to children and to prepare young people and new believers for the Lord's Supper. We believe that these teachings are all Biblical, and are an excellent summary of Bible truth.

Another recitation is next in the outline, and are varied each week. One of several of the following is given – either the Apostles' Creed, the Nicene Creed, the Ten Commandments, or the Heidelberg Catechism Q&A # 1. You probably know some of these, but the last one may be less familiar. Trust me, and just read it over a few times. You will soon see how powerful it is, and how blessed is the man, woman, or child who memorizes it!

After that is a section for prayer requests. You will notice that I broke them down into three main categories; family, church, and world. These are all blank and ready for you to fill in. Go ahead and make them personal. If you jot down a few prayer requests under those headings, you have probably covered most of the main petitions and needs in your life.

Following is the Lord's Prayer. This hardly needs any introduction. I still love to pray through the simple and sublime prayer that Jesus gave His disciples in the Gospels of Matthew and Luke. We never outgrow that prayer. Don't tire of it. I should also mention that the Lord's Prayer and the Ten Commandments are given in the King James Version (Authorized Version) in order to retain the traditional language.

About music: If you would like to sing as a family, I would urge you to go ahead and do so. Personally, I have found the Scottish Psalter in meter to be a wonderful thing to sing aloud. It is, after all, the Word of God (the Psalms) set to rhyme and meter so that you can sing it with any common meter tune such as *Amazing Grace, O For a Thousand Tongues to Sing,* or *I Sing the Mighty Power of God.* If that doesn't appeal to you, perhaps you could use the church hymnal if you have a copy. Or, even simpler, use a playlist on Youtube, and sing a current praise songs from your phone or device.

Then you will find some blank space added towards the end. Use this however you want. I could see families practicing writing some letters and easy words for kids who are learning to read. Or more advanced children could write out a catechism answer. Anyone with an artistic mind could draw a simple sketch of something discussed in the sermon or the devotion. Do whatever you want there. The canvas is blank. Feel free to come up with your own ideas.

Finally, and this is the last bit, go out and have some fun together. I have put a weekly reminder at the end of every devotion to do something as a family. I made a brief list of about thirty things to do as a family in Appendix #1. Take them in any order you want. Some are inside games and others are for outdoors. Just promise not to stare at screens all day, alright?

A Word about Repetition and Creativity

Some people probably won't like this devotional because it is repetitive. I understand that. Yes, the prayers at the beginning are all the identical, and the creeds are pretty much repeated throughout. But don't forget that repetition is a good thing. Just look at the regularity of the solar system, or at some of your circulatory body systems that God designed. There is order, regularity, and repetition in all that God made. We do, after all, want our children to learn these things and learn them well. As "big people," we never grow out of them either. They simply deepen in meaning for us as we grow in faith and understanding.

At the same time, there is great freedom here in this book. If you launch into a long discussion about something you read in the Scripture text and never finish the section, I count that as a good thing. Take the conversation where you want it to go. Let the Spirit guide you. I purposefully tried to make this devotional as flexible as possible so that you are not restrained to "get through the material" each week. That way, you can discuss whatever you want about the text or the ancient words reprinted in this book.

Have fun. Draw close to one another. And remember to meet with Jesus at the table.

Dr. Matthew Everhard
Fall 2019

✋ **Opening Prayer (from the Book of Common Prayer). All pray together, or head of household may lead.**

Almighty God, to whom all hearts are open, all desires known, and from whom no secrets are hid; cleanse the thoughts of our hearts by the inspiration of Thy Holy Spirit, that we may more perfectly love Thee, and more worthily magnify Thy holy name, through Jesus Christ our Lord, Amen.

📖 **Scripture Reading: Mark 1:1-11 (ESV)**

1 The beginning of the gospel of Jesus Christ, the Son of God.
2 As it is written in Isaiah the prophet,
"Behold, I send my messenger before your face,
    who will prepare your way,
3 the voice of one crying in the wilderness:
    'Prepare the way of the Lord,
    make his paths straight,'"
4 John appeared, baptizing in the wilderness and proclaiming a baptism of repentance for the forgiveness of sins.**5** And all the country of Judea and all Jerusalem were going out to him and were being baptized by him in the river Jordan, confessing their sins. **6** Now John was clothed with camel's hair and wore a leather belt around his waist and ate locusts and wild honey. **7** And he preached, saying, "After me comes he who is mightier than I, the strap of whose sandals I am not worthy to stoop down and untie. **8** I have baptized you with water, but he will baptize you with the Holy Spirit."
9 In those days Jesus came from Nazareth of Galilee and was baptized by John in the Jordan. **10** And when he came up out of the water, immediately he saw the heavens being torn open and the

Spirit descending on him like a dove. [11] And a voice came from heaven, "You are my beloved Son; with you I am well pleased."

➡ Scripture Reflection on Today's Reading

Put a circle around difficult words and phrases.

Put a star next to verses that cause us to praise and give thanks.

Underline verses with commands or that lead us to repent.

Put a box around key concepts and other family discussion points.

🎓 Westminster Catechism Questions

Q. 1. *What is the chief end of man?*
A. Man's chief end is to glorify God, and to enjoy him forever.

Q. 2. *What rule hath God given to direct us how we may glorify and enjoy him?*
A. The Word of God, which is contained in the Scriptures of the Old and New Testaments, is the only rule to direct us how we may glorify and enjoy him.

🔊 Apostle's Creed: Recite as a Family

I believe in God the Father Almighty, Maker of heaven and earth. I believe in Jesus Christ, His only Son, our Lord, who was conceived by the Holy Spirit, and born of the Virgin Mary. He suffered under Pontius Pilate, was crucified, died, and was buried; he descended into hell. The third day he rose again from the dead. He ascended into heaven, he is seated at the right hand of God the Father Almighty. From there he will come to judge the living and the dead. I believe in the Holy Spirit, the holy catholic church, the communion of saints, the forgiveness of sins, the resurrection of the body, and the life everlasting. Amen.

✋ Prayer Requests of the Week

Our Family

-

-

-

The Church

-

-

-

-

The World

-

-

-

🔊 The Lord's Prayer: Recite Together

Our Father which art in heaven, Hallowed be thy name. Thy kingdom come, Thy will be done in earth, as it is in heaven. Give us this day our daily bread. And forgive us our debts, as we forgive our debtors. And lead us not into temptation, but deliver us from evil: For thine is the kingdom, and the power, and the glory, forever. Amen.

🎵 **Optional Singing:** Select a "psalm, hymn, or spiritual song" (Ephesians 5:19), from the Psalter, the church hymnal, or a Youtube worship playlist.

👉 Exercises For Children

In the free space on this page: (1) write out one of the catechism questions, (2) practice writing out or spelling some of the key words from the Scripture reading, or (3) draw a picture of something important from today's family discussion.

Family Activity Suggestion: Take a walk around the block or family property. See Appendix #1 for other quality time ideas.

SERMON NOTES ON THIS WEEK'S TEXT

DATE

PREACHER

INTRODUCTION

MAIN IDEAS

PERSONAL or FAMILY APPLICATIONS

👆 Opening Prayer (from the Book of Common Prayer). All pray together, or head of household may lead.

Almighty God, to whom all hearts are open, all desires known, and from whom no secrets are hid; cleanse the thoughts of our hearts by the inspiration of Thy Holy Spirit, that we may more perfectly love Thee, and more worthily magnify Thy holy name, through Jesus Christ our Lord, Amen.

📖 Scripture Reading: Mark 1:12-20 (ESV)

[12] The Spirit immediately drove him out into the wilderness. [13] And he was in the wilderness forty days, being tempted by Satan. And he was with the wild animals, and the angels were ministering to him.

[14] Now after John was arrested, Jesus came into Galilee, proclaiming the gospel of God, [15] and saying, "The time is fulfilled, and the kingdom of God is at hand; repent and believe in the gospel."

[16] Passing alongside the Sea of Galilee, he saw Simon and Andrew the brother of Simon casting a net into the sea, for they were fishermen. [17] And Jesus said to them, "Follow me, and I will make you become fishers of men." [18] And immediately they left their nets and followed him. [19] And going on a little farther, he saw James the son of Zebedee and John his brother, who were in their boat mending the nets. [20] And immediately he called them, and they left their father Zebedee in the boat with the hired servants and followed him.

➡ Scripture Reflection on Today's Reading

Put a circle around difficult words and phrases.

Put a star next to verses that cause us to praise and give thanks.

Underline verses with commands or that lead us to repent.

Put a box around key concepts and other family discussion points.

Westminster Catechism Questions

Q. 3. *What do the Scriptures principally teach?*
A. The Scriptures principally teach what man is to believe concerning God, and what duty God requires of man.

Q. 4. *What is God?*
A. God is a spirit, infinite, eternal, and unchangeable, in his being, wisdom, power, holiness, justice, goodness and truth.

🔊 Nicene Creed: Recite as a Family

We believe in one God, the Father Almighty, Maker of heaven and earth, and of all things visible and invisible.
And in one Lord Jesus Christ, the only-begotten Son of God, begotten of the Father before all worlds; God of God, Light of Light, very God of very God; begotten, not made, being of one substance with the Father, by whom all things were made. Who, for us and for our salvation, came down from heaven, and was incarnate by the Holy Spirit of the virgin Mary, and was made man; and was crucified also for us under Pontius Pilate; He suffered and was buried; and the third day He rose again, according to the Scriptures; and ascended into heaven, and sits on the right hand of

the Father; and He shall come again, with glory, to judge the living and the dead; whose kingdom shall have no end.

And we believe in the Holy Ghost, the Lord and Giver of Life, who proceeds from the Father and the Son; who with the Father and the Son together is worshipped and glorified; who spoke by the prophets. And we believe in one holy catholic and apostolic Church. We acknowledge one baptism for the remission of sins; and we look for the resurrection of the dead, and the life of the world to come. Amen.

🖐 Prayer Requests of the Week

Our Family

•

•

•

The Church

•

•

•

The World

•

•

🔊 The Lord's Prayer: Recite Together

Our Father which art in heaven, Hallowed be thy name. Thy kingdom come, Thy will be done in earth, as it is in heaven. Give us this day our daily bread. And forgive us our debts, as we forgive our debtors. And lead us not into temptation, but deliver us from evil: For thine is the kingdom, and the power, and the glory, forever. Amen.

🎵 **Optional Singing:** Select a "psalm, hymn, or spiritual song" (Ephesians 5:19), from the Psalter, the church hymnal, or a Youtube worship playlist.

➾ Exercises For Children
In the free space on this page: (1) write out one of the catechism questions, (2) practice writing out or spelling some of the key words from the Scripture reading, or (3) draw a picture of something important from today's family discussion.

Family Activity Suggestion: Collect leaves around the neighborhood or property and discuss what kinds of trees are growing. See Appendix #1 for other quality time ideas.

SERMON NOTES ON THIS WEEK'S TEXT

DATE

PREACHER

INTRODUCTION

MAIN IDEAS

PERSONAL or FAMILY APPLICATIONS

🖐 **Opening Prayer (from the Book of Common Prayer). All pray together, or head of household may lead.**

Almighty God, to whom all hearts are open, all desires known, and from whom no secrets are hid; cleanse the thoughts of our hearts by the inspiration of Thy Holy Spirit, that we may more perfectly love Thee, and more worthily magnify Thy holy name, through Jesus Christ our Lord, Amen.

📖 **Scripture Reading: Mark 1:21-34 (ESV)**

21 And they went into Capernaum, and immediately on the Sabbath he entered the synagogue and was teaching. 22 And they were astonished at his teaching, for he taught them as one who had authority, and not as the scribes. 23 And immediately there was in their synagogue a man with an unclean spirit. And he cried out, 24 "What have you to do with us, Jesus of Nazareth? Have you come to destroy us? I know who you are—the Holy One of God." 25 But Jesus rebuked him, saying, "Be silent, and come out of him!" 26 And the unclean spirit, convulsing him and crying out with a loud voice, came out of him. 27 And they were all amazed, so that they questioned among themselves, saying, "What is this? A new teaching with authority! He commands even the unclean spirits, and they obey him." 28 And at once his fame spread everywhere throughout all the surrounding region of Galilee.

29 And immediately he left the synagogue and entered the house of Simon and Andrew, with James and John. 30 Now Simon's mother-in-law lay ill with a fever, and immediately they told him about her. 31 And he came and took her by the hand and lifted her up, and the fever left her, and she began to serve them.

[32] That evening at sundown they brought to him all who were sick or oppressed by demons. [33] And the whole city was gathered together at the door. [34] And he healed many who were sick with various diseases, and cast out many demons. And he would not permit the demons to speak, because they knew him.

➥ Scripture Reflection on Today's Reading

Put a circle around difficult words and phrases.

Put a star next to verses that cause us to praise and give thanks.

Underline verses with commands or that lead us to repent.

Put a box around key concepts and other family discussion points.

🎓 Westminster Catechism Questions

Q. 5. *Are there more Gods than one?*
A. There is but one only, the living and true God.

Q. 6. *How many persons are there in the godhead?*
A. There are three persons in the Godhead; the Father, the Son, and the Holy Ghost; and these three are one God, the same in substance, equal in power and glory.

◀ Ten Commandments: Recite as a Family

And God spake all these words, saying,
I am the Lord thy God, which have brought thee out of the land of Egypt, out of the house of bondage.
1. Thou shalt have no other gods before me.
2. Thou shalt not make unto thee any graven image, or any likeness of any thing that is in heaven above, or that is in the

earth beneath, or that is in the water under the earth. Thou shalt not bow down thyself to them, nor serve them: for I the Lord thy God am a jealous God, visiting the iniquity of the fathers upon the children unto the third and fourth generation of them that hate me; And shewing mercy unto thousands of them that love me, and keep my commandments.

3. Thou shalt not take the name of the Lord thy God in vain; for the Lord will not hold him guiltless that taketh his name in vain.

4. Remember the sabbath day, to keep it holy. Six days shalt thou labour, and do all thy work: But the seventh day is the sabbath of the Lord thy God: in it thou shalt not do any work, thou, nor thy son, nor thy daughter, thy manservant, nor thy maidservant, nor thy cattle, nor thy stranger that is within thy gates: For in six days the Lord made heaven and earth, the sea, and all that in them is, and rested the seventh day: wherefore the Lord blessed the sabbath day, and hallowed it.

5. Honour thy father and thy mother: that thy days may be long upon the land which the Lord thy God giveth thee.

6. Thou shalt not kill.

7. Thou shalt not commit adultery.

8. Thou shalt not steal.

9. Thou shalt not bear false witness against thy neighbour.

10. Thou shalt not covet thy neighbour's house, thou shalt not covet thy neighbour's wife, nor his manservant, nor his maidservant, nor his ox, nor his ass, nor any thing that is thy neighbour's.

🖐 Prayer Requests of the Week

Our Family

-

-

-

The Church

-

-

-

The World

-

-

-

🔊 The Lord's Prayer: Recite Together

Our Father which art in heaven, Hallowed be thy name. Thy kingdom come, Thy will be done in earth, as it is in heaven. Give us this day our daily bread. And forgive us our debts, as we forgive our debtors. And lead us not into temptation, but deliver us from evil: For thine is the kingdom, and the power, and the glory, forever. Amen.

🎵 **Optional Singing:** Select a "psalm, hymn, or spiritual song" (Ephesians 5:19), from the Psalter, the church hymnal, or a Youtube worship playlist.

➤ Exercises For Children

In the free space on this page: (1) write out one of the catechism questions, (2) practice writing out or spelling some of the key words from the Scripture reading, or (3) draw a picture of something important from today's family discussion.

Family Activity Suggestion: Write a family 'thank you' letter to someone who has shown love or encouragement to you as a family. See Appendix #1 for other quality time ideas.

SERMON NOTES ON THIS WEEK'S TEXT

DATE

PREACHER

INTRODUCTION

MAIN IDEAS

PERSONAL or FAMILY APPLICATIONS

♨ Call to Worship, Psalm 95 KJV
(Traditionally called the Venite Exultemus Domino)

[1] O come, let us sing unto the Lord: let us make a joyful noise to the rock of our salvation. [2] Let us come before his presence with thanksgiving, and make a joyful noise unto him with psalms. [3] For the Lord is a great God, and a great King above all gods. [4] In his hand are the deep places of the earth: the strength of the hills is his also. [5] The sea is his, and he made it: and his hands formed the dry land. [6] O come, let us worship and bow down: let us kneel before the Lord our maker. [7] For he is our God; and we are the people of his pasture, and the sheep of his hand.

📖 Scripture Reading: Mark 1:35-45 (ESV)

[35] And rising very early in the morning, while it was still dark, he departed and went out to a desolate place, and there he prayed. [36] And Simon and those who were with him searched for him, [37] and they found him and said to him, "Everyone is looking for you." [38] And he said to them, "Let us go on to the next towns, that I may preach there also, for that is why I came out." [39] And he went throughout all Galilee, preaching in their synagogues and casting out demons.
[40] And a leper came to him, imploring him, and kneeling said to him, "If you will, you can make me clean." [41] Moved with pity, he stretched out his hand and touched him and said to him, "I will; be clean."[42] And immediately the leprosy left him, and he was made clean. [43] And Jesus sternly charged him and sent him away at once, [44] and said to him, "See that you say nothing to anyone, but go, show yourself to the priest and offer for your cleansing what Moses commanded, for a proof to them." [45] But he went out and began to talk freely about it, and to spread the news, so that Jesus

could no longer openly enter a town, but was out in desolate places, and people were coming to him from every quarter.

➡ Scripture Reflection on Today's Reading

Put a circle around difficult words and phrases.

Put a star next to verses that cause us to praise and give thanks.

Underline verses with commands or that lead us to repent.

Put a box around key concepts and other family discussion points.

🎓 Westminster Catechism Questions

Q. 7. *What are the decrees of God?*
A. The decrees of God are his eternal purpose, according to the counsel of his will, whereby, for his own glory, he hath foreordained whatsoever comes to pass.

Q. 8. *How doth God execute his decrees?*
A. God executeth his decrees in the works of creation and providence.

🔊 Heidelberg Catechism Question #1

Question 1. What is thy only comfort in life and death?

Answer: That I with body and soul, both in life and death, am not my own, but belong unto my faithful Saviour Jesus Christ; who, with his precious blood, has fully satisfied for all my sins, and delivered me from all the power of the devil; and so preserves me that without the will of my heavenly Father, not a hair can fall from my head; yea, that all things must be subservient to my salvation, and therefore, by his Holy Spirit, He also assures me of eternal life, and makes me sincerely willing and ready, henceforth, to live unto him.

 Optional Singing: Select a "psalm, hymn, or spiritual song" (Ephesians 5:19), from the Psalter, the church hymnal, or a Youtube worship playlist.

✋ Prayer Requests of the Week

Our Family

-
-
-

The Church

-
-
-

The World

-
-
-

🔊 The Lord's Prayer: Recite Together

Our Father which art in heaven, Hallowed be thy name. Thy kingdom come, Thy will be done in earth, as it is in heaven. Give us this day our daily bread. And forgive us our debts, as we forgive our debtors. And lead us not into temptation, but deliver us from evil: For thine is the kingdom, and the power, and the glory, forever. Amen.

🎵 **Optional Singing:** Select a "psalm, hymn, or spiritual song" (Ephesians 5:19), from the Psalter, the church hymnal, or a Youtube worship playlist.

🔖 Exercises For Children

In the free space on this page: (1) write out one of the catechism questions, (2) practice writing out or spelling some of the key words from the Scripture reading, or (3) draw a picture of something important from today's family discussion.

Family Activity Suggestion: Prepare a meal or tasty snack for a neighbor or shut-in from our church. See Appendix #1 for other quality time ideas.

SERMON NOTES ON THIS WEEK'S TEXT

DATE

PREACHER

INTRODUCTION

MAIN IDEAS

PERSONAL or FAMILY APPLICATIONS

🖐 **Opening Prayer (from the Book of Common Prayer). All pray together, or head of household may lead.**

Almighty God, to whom all hearts are open, all desires known, and from whom no secrets are hid; cleanse the thoughts of our hearts by the inspiration of Thy Holy Spirit, that we may more perfectly love Thee, and more worthily magnify Thy holy name, through Jesus Christ our Lord, Amen.

📖 **Scripture Reading: Mark 2:1-12 (ESV)**

And when he returned to Capernaum after some days, it was reported that he was at home. [2] And many were gathered together, so that there was no more room, not even at the door. And he was preaching the word to them. [3] And they came, bringing to him a paralytic carried by four men. [4] And when they could not get near him because of the crowd, they removed the roof above him, and when they had made an opening, they let down the bed on which the paralytic lay. [5] And when Jesus saw their faith, he said to the paralytic, "Son, your sins are forgiven." [6] Now some of the scribes were sitting there, questioning in their hearts, [7] "Why does this man speak like that? He is blaspheming! Who can forgive sins but God alone?" [8] And immediately Jesus, perceiving in his spirit that they thus questioned within themselves, said to them, "Why do you question these things in your hearts? [9] Which is easier, to say to the paralytic, 'Your sins are forgiven,' or to say, 'Rise, take up your bed and walk'? [10] But that you may know that the Son of Man has authority on earth to forgive sins"—he said to the paralytic— [11] "I say to you, rise, pick up your bed, and go home." [12] And he rose and immediately picked up his bed and went out before them all, so that they were all amazed and glorified God, saying, "We never saw anything like this!"

✏ Scripture Reflection on Today's Reading

Put a circle around difficult words and phrases.

Put a star next to verses that cause us to praise and give thanks.

Underline verses with commands or that lead us to repent.

Put a box around key concepts and other family discussion points.

🎓 Westminster Catechism Questions

Q. 9. *What is the work of creation?*
A. The work of creation is God's making all things of nothing, by the word of his power, in the space of six days, and all very good.

Q. 10. *How did God create man?*
A. God created man male and female, after his own image, in knowledge, righteousness and holiness, with dominion over the creatures.

🔊 Apostle's Creed: Recite as a Family

I believe in God the Father Almighty, Maker of heaven and earth. I believe in Jesus Christ, His only Son, our Lord, who was conceived by the Holy Spirit, and born of the Virgin Mary. He suffered under Pontius Pilate, was crucified, died, and was buried; he descended into hell. The third day he rose again from the dead. He ascended into heaven, he is seated at the right hand of God the Father Almighty. From there he will come to judge the living and the dead. I believe in the Holy Spirit, the holy catholic church, the communion of saints, the forgiveness of sins, the resurrection of the body, and the life everlasting. Amen.

👆 Prayer Requests of the Week

Our Family

*

*

*

The Church

*

*

*

The World

*

*

*

🔊 The Lord's Prayer: Recite Together

Our Father which art in heaven, Hallowed be thy name. Thy kingdom come, Thy will be done in earth, as it is in heaven. Give us this day our daily bread. And forgive us our debts, as we forgive our debtors. And lead us not into temptation, but deliver us from evil:

For thine is the kingdom, and the power, and the glory, forever. Amen.

🎵 **Optional Singing:** Select a "psalm, hymn, or spiritual song" (Ephesians 5:19), from the Psalter, the church hymnal, or a Youtube worship playlist.

🖝 **Exercises For Children**
In the free space on this page: (1) write out one of the catechism questions, (2) practice writing out or spelling some of the key words from the Scripture reading, or (3) draw a picture of something important from today's family discussion.

Family Activity Suggestion: Get out your family photo albums and take some time thinking of fond memories with loved ones. See Appendix #1 for other quality time ideas.

SERMON NOTES ON THIS WEEK'S TEXT

DATE

PREACHER

INTRODUCTION

MAIN IDEAS

PERSONAL or FAMILY APPLICATIONS

🖐 Opening Prayer (from the Book of Common Prayer). All pray together, or head of household may lead.

Almighty God, to whom all hearts are open, all desires known, and from whom no secrets are hid; cleanse the thoughts of our hearts by the inspiration of Thy Holy Spirit, that we may more perfectly love Thee, and more worthily magnify Thy holy name, through Jesus Christ our Lord, Amen.

📖 Scripture Reading: Mark 2:13-17 (ESV)

[13] He went out again beside the sea, and all the crowd was coming to him, and he was teaching them. [14] And as he passed by, he saw Levi the son of Alphaeus sitting at the tax booth, and he said to him, "Follow me." And he rose and followed him.
[15] And as he reclined at table in his house, many tax collectors and sinners were reclining with Jesus and his disciples, for there were many who followed him.[16] And the scribes of the Pharisees, when they saw that he was eating with sinners and tax collectors, said to his disciples, "Why does he eat with tax collectors and sinners?" [17] And when Jesus heard it, he said to them, "Those who are well have no need of a physician, but those who are sick. I came not to call the righteous, but sinners."

☞ Scripture Reflection on Today's Reading

Put a circle around difficult words and phrases.

Put a star next to verses that cause us to praise and give thanks.

Underline verses with commands or that lead us to repent.

Put a box around key concepts and other family discussion points.

Westminster Catechism Questions

Q. 11. *What are God's works of providence?*
A. God's works of providence are his most holy, wise and powerful preserving and governing all his creatures, and all their actions.

Q. 12. *What special act of providence did God exercise toward man in the estate wherein he was created?*
A. When God had created man, he entered into a covenant of life with him, upon condition of perfect obedience; forbidding him to eat of the tree of the knowledge of good and evil, upon pain of death.

◀)) Nicene Creed: Recite as a Family

We believe in one God, the Father Almighty, Maker of heaven and earth, and of all things visible and invisible.
And in one Lord Jesus Christ, the only-begotten Son of God, begotten of the Father before all worlds; God of God, Light of Light, very God of very God; begotten, not made, being of one substance with the Father, by whom all things were made. Who, for us and for our salvation, came down from heaven, and was incarnate by the Holy Spirit of the virgin Mary, and was made man; and was crucified also for us under Pontius Pilate; He suffered and was buried; and the third day He rose again, according to the Scriptures; and ascended into heaven, and sits on the right hand of the Father; and He shall come again, with glory, to judge the living and the dead; whose kingdom shall have no end.
And we believe in the Holy Ghost, the Lord and Giver of Life, who proceeds from the Father and the Son; who with the Father and the Son together is worshipped and glorified; who spoke by the prophets. And we believe in one holy catholic and apostolic Church. We acknowledge one baptism for the remission of sins; and we

look for the resurrection of the dead, and the life of the world to come. Amen.

✋ Prayer Requests of the Week

Our Family

-

-

-

The Church

-

-

-

The World

-

-

-

🔊 The Lord's Prayer: Recite Together

Our Father which art in heaven, Hallowed be thy name. Thy kingdom come, Thy will be done in earth, as it is in heaven. Give us this day our daily bread. And forgive us our debts, as we forgive our

debtors. And lead us not into temptation, but deliver us from evil: For thine is the kingdom, and the power, and the glory, forever. Amen.

🎵 **Optional Singing:** Select a "psalm, hymn, or spiritual song" (Ephesians 5:19), from the Psalter, the church hymnal, or a Youtube worship playlist.

➥ Exercises For Children
In the free space on this page: (1) write out one of the catechism questions, (2) practice writing out or spelling some of the key words from the Scripture reading, or (3) draw a picture of something important from today's family discussion.

Family Activity Suggestion: Create a simple 'family tree' craft and learn about your relatives, living and in the past.
See Appendix #1 for other quality time ideas.

SERMON NOTES ON THIS WEEK'S TEXT

DATE

PREACHER

INTRODUCTION

MAIN IDEAS

PERSONAL or FAMILY APPLICATIONS

🕯 Opening Prayer (from the Book of Common Prayer). All pray together, or head of household may lead.

Almighty God, to whom all hearts are open, all desires known, and from whom no secrets are hid; cleanse the thoughts of our hearts by the inspiration of Thy Holy Spirit, that we may more perfectly love Thee, and more worthily magnify Thy holy name, through Jesus Christ our Lord, Amen.

📖 Scripture Reading: Mark 2:18-28 (ESV)

[18] Now John's disciples and the Pharisees were fasting. And people came and said to him, "Why do John's disciples and the disciples of the Pharisees fast, but your disciples do not fast?" [19] And Jesus said to them, "Can the wedding guests fast while the bridegroom is with them? As long as they have the bridegroom with them, they cannot fast. [20] The days will come when the bridegroom is taken away from them, and then they will fast in that day. [21] No one sews a piece of unshrunk cloth on an old garment. If he does, the patch tears away from it, the new from the old, and a worse tear is made. [22] And no one puts new wine into old wineskins. If he does, the wine will burst the skins—and the wine is destroyed, and so are the skins. But new wine is for fresh wineskins."

[23] One Sabbath he was going through the grainfields, and as they made their way, his disciples began to pluck heads of grain. [24] And the Pharisees were saying to him, "Look, why are they doing what is not lawful on the Sabbath?" [25] And he said to them, "Have you never read what David did, when he was in need and was hungry, he and those who were with him: [26] how he entered the house of God, in the time of Abiathar the high priest, and ate the bread of the Presence, which it is not lawful for any but the priests to eat, and

also gave it to those who were with him?"[27] And he said to them, "The Sabbath was made for man, not man for the Sabbath.[28] So the Son of Man is lord even of the Sabbath."

➤ Scripture Reflection on Today's Reading

Put a circle around difficult words and phrases.

Put a star next to verses that cause us to praise and give thanks.

Underline verses with commands or that lead us to repent.

Put a box around key concepts and other family discussion points.

🎓 Westminster Catechism Questions

Q. 13. *Did our first parents continue in the estate wherein they were created?*
A. Our first parents, being left to the freedom of their own will, fell from the estate wherein they were created, by sinning against God.

Q. 14. *What is sin?*
A. Sin is any want of conformity unto, or transgression of, the law of God.

🔊 Ten Commandments: Recite as a Family

And God spake all these words, saying,
I am the Lord thy God, which have brought thee out of the land of Egypt, out of the house of bondage.
1. Thou shalt have no other gods before me.
2. Thou shalt not make unto thee any graven image, or any likeness of any thing that is in heaven above, or that is in the earth beneath, or that is in the water under the earth. Thou

shalt not bow down thyself to them, nor serve them: for I the Lord thy God am a jealous God, visiting the iniquity of the fathers upon the children unto the third and fourth generation of them that hate me; And shewing mercy unto thousands of them that love me, and keep my commandments.

3. Thou shalt not take the name of the Lord thy God in vain; for the Lord will not hold him guiltless that taketh his name in vain.

4. Remember the sabbath day, to keep it holy. Six days shalt thou labour, and do all thy work: But the seventh day is the sabbath of the Lord thy God: in it thou shalt not do any work, thou, nor thy son, nor thy daughter, thy manservant, nor thy maidservant, nor thy cattle, nor thy stranger that is within thy gates: For in six days the Lord made heaven and earth, the sea, and all that in them is, and rested the seventh day: wherefore the Lord blessed the sabbath day, and hallowed it.

5. Honour thy father and thy mother: that thy days may be long upon the land which the Lord thy God giveth thee.

6. Thou shalt not kill.

7. Thou shalt not commit adultery.

8. Thou shalt not steal.

9. Thou shalt not bear false witness against thy neighbour.

10. Thou shalt not covet thy neighbour's house, thou shalt not covet thy neighbour's wife, nor his manservant, nor his maidservant, nor his ox, nor his ass, nor any thing that is thy neighbour's.

✋ Prayer Requests of the Week

Our Family

•

-

-

The Church

-

-

-

The World

-

-

-

🔊 **The Lord's Prayer: Recite Together**

Our Father which art in heaven, Hallowed be thy name. Thy kingdom come, Thy will be done in earth, as it is in heaven. Give us this day our daily bread. And forgive us our debts, as we forgive our debtors. And lead us not into temptation, but deliver us from evil: For thine is the kingdom, and the power, and the glory, forever. Amen.

🎵 **Optional Singing:** Select a "psalm, hymn, or spiritual song" (Ephesians 5:19), from the Psalter, the church hymnal, or a Youtube worship playlist.

➤ Exercises For Children

In the free space on this page: (1) write out one of the catechism questions, (2) practice writing out or spelling some of the key words from the Scripture reading, or (3) draw a picture of something important from today's family discussion.

Family Activity Suggestion: Paint some small rocks and place them in public places for people to discover. Join a rock painting group on Facebook to see who finds and posts your rocks! See Appendix #1 for other quality time ideas.

SERMON NOTES ON THIS WEEK'S TEXT

DATE

PREACHER

INTRODUCTION

MAIN IDEAS

PERSONAL or FAMILY APPLICATIONS

🖐 Call to Worship, Psalm 95 KJV
(Traditionally called the Venite Exultemus Domino)

[1] O come, let us sing unto the Lord: let us make a joyful noise to the rock of our salvation. [2] Let us come before his presence with thanksgiving, and make a joyful noise unto him with psalms. [3] For the Lord is a great God, and a great King above all gods. [4] In his hand are the deep places of the earth: the strength of the hills is his also. [5] The sea is his, and he made it: and his hands formed the dry land. [6] O come, let us worship and bow down: let us kneel before the Lord our maker. [7] For he is our God; and we are the people of his pasture, and the sheep of his hand.

📕 Scripture Reading: Mark 3:1-12 (ESV)

Again he entered the synagogue, and a man was there with a withered hand. [2] And they watched Jesus, to see whether he would heal him on the Sabbath, so that they might accuse him. [3] And he said to the man with the withered hand, "Come here." [4] And he said to them, "Is it lawful on the Sabbath to do good or to do harm, to save life or to kill?" But they were silent. [5] And he looked around at them with anger, grieved at their hardness of heart, and said to the man, "Stretch out your hand." He stretched it out, and his hand was restored. [6] The Pharisees went out and immediately held counsel with the Herodians against him, how to destroy him.

[7] Jesus withdrew with his disciples to the sea, and a great crowd followed, from Galilee and Judea [8] and Jerusalem and Idumea and from beyond the Jordan and from around Tyre and Sidon. When the great crowd heard all that he was doing, they came to him. [9] And he told his disciples to have a boat ready for him because of the crowd, lest they crush him, [10] for he had healed

47

many, so that all who had diseases pressed around him to touch him. **11** And whenever the unclean spirits saw him, they fell down before him and cried out, "You are the Son of God." **12** And he strictly ordered them not to make him known.

➥ Scripture Reflection on Today's Reading

Put a circle around difficult words and phrases.

Put a star next to verses that cause us to praise and give thanks.

Underline verses with commands or that lead us to repent.

Put a box around key concepts and other family discussion points.

🎓 Westminster Catechism Questions

Q. 15. *What was the sin whereby our first parents fell from the estate wherein they were created?*
A. The sin whereby our first parents fell from the estate wherein they were created was their eating the forbidden fruit.

Q. 16. *Did all mankind fall in Adam's first transgression?*
A. The covenant being made with Adam, not only for himself, but for his posterity; all mankind, descending from him by ordinary generation, sinned in him, and fell with him, in his first transgression.

🔊 Heidelberg Catechism Question #1

Question 1. What is thy only comfort in life and death?

Answer: That I with body and soul, both in life and death, am not my own, but belong unto my faithful Saviour Jesus Christ; who, with his precious blood, has fully satisfied for all my sins, and delivered me from all the power of the devil; and so preserves me that without the will of my heavenly Father, not a hair can fall from my head; yea, that all things must be subservient to my salvation, and therefore, by his Holy Spirit, He also assures me of eternal life, and makes me sincerely willing and ready, henceforth, to live unto him.

✋ Prayer Requests of the Week

Our Family

*

*

*

The Church

*

*

*

The World

*

*

*

🔊 The Lord's Prayer: Recite Together

Our Father which art in heaven, Hallowed be thy name. Thy kingdom come, Thy will be done in earth, as it is in heaven. Give us this day our daily bread. And forgive us our debts, as we forgive our debtors. And lead us not into temptation, but deliver us from evil: For thine is the kingdom, and the power, and the glory, forever. Amen.

🎜 **Optional Singing:** Select a "psalm, hymn, or spiritual song" (Ephesians 5:19), from the Psalter, the church hymnal, or a Youtube worship playlist.

➡ **Exercises For Children**
In the free space on this page: (1) write out one of the catechism questions, (2) practice writing out or spelling some of the key words from the Scripture reading, or (3) draw a picture of something important from today's family discussion.

Family Activity Suggestion: Read aloud some classic short stories, or read from books that you loved when you were a child. See Appendix #1 for other quality time ideas.

SERMON NOTES ON THIS WEEK'S TEXT

DATE

PREACHER

INTRODUCTION

MAIN IDEAS

PERSONAL or FAMILY APPLICATIONS

🕯 Opening Prayer (from the Book of Common Prayer). All pray together, or head of household may lead.

Almighty God, to whom all hearts are open, all desires known, and from whom no secrets are hid; cleanse the thoughts of our hearts by the inspiration of Thy Holy Spirit, that we may more perfectly love Thee, and more worthily magnify Thy holy name, through Jesus Christ our Lord, Amen.

📖 Scripture Reading: Mark 3:13-30 (ESV)

[13] And he went up on the mountain and called to him those whom he desired, and they came to him. [14] And he appointed twelve (whom he also named apostles) so that they might be with him and he might send them out to preach[15] and have authority to cast out demons. [16] He appointed the twelve: Simon (to whom he gave the name Peter); [17] James the son of Zebedee and John the brother of James (to whom he gave the name Boanerges, that is, Sons of Thunder); [18] Andrew, and Philip, and Bartholomew, and Matthew, and Thomas, and James the son of Alphaeus, and Thaddaeus, and Simon the Zealot, [19] and Judas Iscariot, who betrayed him. [20] Then he went home, and the crowd gathered again, so that they could not even eat. [21] And when his family heard it, they went out to seize him, for they were saying, "He is out of his mind."

[22] And the scribes who came down from Jerusalem were saying, "He is possessed by Beelzebul," and "by the prince of demons he casts out the demons." [23] And he called them to him and said to them in parables, "How can Satan cast out Satan? [24] If a kingdom is divided against itself, that kingdom cannot stand.[25] And if a house is divided against itself, that house will not

be able to stand.[26] And if Satan has risen up against himself and is divided, he cannot stand, but is coming to an end. [27] But no one can enter a strong man's house and plunder his goods, unless he first binds the strong man. Then indeed he may plunder his house. [28] "Truly, I say to you, all sins will be forgiven the children of man, and whatever blasphemies they utter, [29] but whoever blasphemes against the Holy Spirit never has forgiveness, but is guilty of an eternal sin"— [30] for they were saying, "He has an unclean spirit."

✏ Scripture Reflection on Today's Reading

Put a circle around difficult words and phrases.

Put a star next to verses that cause us to praise and give thanks.

Underline verses with commands or that lead us to repent.

Put a box around key concepts and other family discussion points.

🎓 Westminster Catechism Questions

Q. 17. *Into what estate did the fall bring mankind?*
A. The fall brought mankind into an estate of sin and misery.

Q. 18. *Wherein consists the sinfulness of that estate whereinto man fell?*
A. The sinfulness of that estate whereinto man fell consists in the guilt of Adam's first sin, the want of original righteousness, and the corruption of his whole nature, which is commonly called original sin; together with all actual transgressions which proceed from it.

🔊 Apostle's Creed: Recite as a Family

I believe in God the Father Almighty, Maker of heaven and earth. I believe in Jesus Christ, His only Son, our Lord, who was conceived by the Holy Spirit, and born of the Virgin Mary. He suffered under Pontius Pilate, was crucified, died, and was buried; he descended into hell. The third day he rose again from the dead. He ascended into heaven, he is seated at the right hand of God the Father Almighty. From there he will come to judge the living and the dead. I believe in the Holy Spirit, the holy catholic church, the communion of saints, the forgiveness of sins, the resurrection of the body, and the life everlasting. Amen.

✋ Prayer Requests of the Week

Our Family

-

-

-

The Church

-

-

The World

-

-

●

🔊 The Lord's Prayer: Recite Together

Our Father which art in heaven, Hallowed be thy name. Thy kingdom come, Thy will be done in earth, as it is in heaven. Give us this day our daily bread. And forgive us our debts, as we forgive our debtors. And lead us not into temptation, but deliver us from evil: For thine is the kingdom, and the power, and the glory, forever. Amen.

🎵 **Optional Singing:** Select a "psalm, hymn, or spiritual song" (Ephesians 5:19), from the Psalter, the church hymnal, or a Youtube worship playlist.

✏ Exercises For Children
In the free space on this page: (1) write out one of the catechism questions, (2) practice writing out or spelling some of the key words from the Scripture reading, or (3) draw a picture of something important from today's family discussion.

Family Activity Suggestion: Tell the story of each child's birth, or about their adoption. If no children are present, tell of your own birth or childhood. See Appendix #1 for other quality time ideas.

SERMON NOTES ON THIS WEEK'S TEXT

DATE

PREACHER

INTRODUCTION

MAIN IDEAS

PERSONAL or FAMILY APPLICATIONS

🔥 **Opening Prayer (from the Book of Common Prayer). All pray together, or head of household may lead.**

Almighty God, to whom all hearts are open, all desires known, and from whom no secrets are hid; cleanse the thoughts of our hearts by the inspiration of Thy Holy Spirit, that we may more perfectly love Thee, and more worthily magnify Thy holy name, through Jesus Christ our Lord, Amen.

📖 **Scripture Reading: Mark 3:31-35 (ESV)**

[31] And his mother and his brothers came, and standing outside they sent to him and called him. [32] And a crowd was sitting around him, and they said to him, "Your mother and your brothers are outside, seeking you." [33] And he answered them, "Who are my mother and my brothers?" [34] And looking about at those who sat around him, he said, "Here are my mother and my brothers! [35] For whoever does the will of God, he is my brother and sister and mother."

📣 **Scripture Reflection on Today's Reading**

Put a circle around difficult words and phrases.

Put a star next to verses that cause us to praise and give thanks.

Underline verses with commands or that lead us to repent.

Put a box around key concepts and other family discussion points.

🎓 Westminster Catechism Questions

Q. 19. *What is the misery of that estate whereinto man fell?*
A. All mankind by their fall lost communion with God, are under his wrath and curse, and so made liable to all miseries in this life, to death itself, and to the pains of hell forever.

Q. 20. *Did God leave all mankind to perish in the estate of sin and misery?*
A. God having, out of his mere good pleasure, from all eternity, elected some to everlasting life, did enter into a covenant of grace, to deliver them out of the estate of sin and misery, and to bring them into an estate of salvation by a redeemer.

🔊 Nicene Creed: Recite as a Family

We believe in one God, the Father Almighty, Maker of heaven and earth, and of all things visible and invisible.
And in one Lord Jesus Christ, the only-begotten Son of God, begotten of the Father before all worlds; God of God, Light of Light, very God of very God; begotten, not made, being of one substance with the Father, by whom all things were made. Who, for us and for our salvation, came down from heaven, and was incarnate by the Holy Spirit of the virgin Mary, and was made man; and was crucified also for us under Pontius Pilate; He suffered and was buried; and the third day He rose again, according to the Scriptures; and ascended into heaven, and sits on the right hand of the Father; and He shall come again, with glory, to judge the living and the dead; whose kingdom shall have no end.
And we believe in the Holy Ghost, the Lord and Giver of Life, who proceeds from the Father and the Son; who with the Father and the Son together is worshipped and glorified; who spoke by the prophets. And we believe in one holy catholic and apostolic Church. We acknowledge one baptism for the remission of sins; and we

look for the resurrection of the dead, and the life of the world to come. Amen.

✋ Prayer Requests of the Week

Our Family

-

-

-

The Church

-

-

-

The World

-

-

-

◀» The Lord's Prayer: Recite Together

Our Father which art in heaven, Hallowed be thy name. Thy kingdom come, Thy will be done in earth, as it is in heaven. Give us this day our daily bread. And forgive us our debts, as we forgive our

debtors. And lead us not into temptation, but deliver us from evil:
For thine is the kingdom, and the power, and the glory, forever.
Amen.

🎵 **Optional Singing:** Select a "psalm, hymn, or spiritual song"
(Ephesians 5:19), from the Psalter, the church hymnal, or a
Youtube worship playlist.

➖ **Exercises For Children**
In the free space on this page: (1) write out one of the catechism
questions, (2) practice writing out or spelling some of the key words
from the Scripture reading, or (3) draw a picture of something
important from today's family discussion.

**Family Activity Suggestion: Create a simple treasure hunt with
map and clues. See Appendix #1 for other quality time ideas.**

SERMON NOTES ON THIS WEEK'S TEXT

DATE

PREACHER

INTRODUCTION

MAIN IDEAS

PERSONAL or FAMILY APPLICATIONS

🤚 Opening Prayer (from the Book of Common Prayer). All pray together, or head of household may lead.

Almighty God, to whom all hearts are open, all desires known, and from whom no secrets are hid; cleanse the thoughts of our hearts by the inspiration of Thy Holy Spirit, that we may more perfectly love Thee, and more worthily magnify Thy holy name, through Jesus Christ our Lord, Amen.

📖 Scripture Reading: Mark 4:1-20 (ESV)

Again he began to teach beside the sea. And a very large crowd gathered about him, so that he got into a boat and sat in it on the sea, and the whole crowd was beside the sea on the land. [2] And he was teaching them many things in parables, and in his teaching he said to them: [3] "Listen! Behold, a sower went out to sow. [4] And as he sowed, some seed fell along the path, and the birds came and devoured it. [5] Other seed fell on rocky ground, where it did not have much soil, and immediately it sprang up, since it had no depth of soil. [6] And when the sun rose, it was scorched, and since it had no root, it withered away. [7] Other seed fell among thorns, and the thorns grew up and choked it, and it yielded no grain. [8] And other seeds fell into good soil and produced grain, growing up and increasing and yielding thirtyfold and sixtyfold and a hundredfold." [9] And he said, "He who has ears to hear, let him hear."

[10] And when he was alone, those around him with the twelve asked him about the parables. [11] And he said to them, "To you has been given the secret of the kingdom of God, but for those outside everything is in parables, [12] so that

"'they may indeed see but not perceive,
    and may indeed hear but not understand,
lest they should turn and be forgiven.'"

[13] And he said to them, "Do you not understand this parable? How then will you understand all the parables? [14] The sower sows the word. [15] And these are the ones along the path, where the word is sown: when they hear, Satan immediately comes and takes away the word that is sown in them. [16] And these are the ones sown on rocky ground: the ones who, when they hear the word, immediately receive it with joy. [17] And they have no root in themselves, but endure for a while; then, when tribulation or persecution arises on account of the word, immediately they fall away. [18] And others are the ones sown among thorns. They are those who hear the word, [19] but the cares of the world and the deceitfulness of riches and the desires for other things enter in and choke the word, and it proves unfruitful. [20] But those that were sown on the good soil are the ones who hear the word and accept it and bear fruit, thirtyfold and sixtyfold and a hundredfold."

⬤ Scripture Reflection on Today's Reading

Put a circle around difficult words and phrases.

Put a star next to verses that cause us to praise and give thanks.

Underline verses with commands or that lead us to repent.

Put a box around key concepts and other family discussion points.

🎓 Westminster Catechism Questions

Q. 21. *Who is the redeemer of God's elect?*
A. The only redeemer of God's elect is the Lord Jesus Christ, who,

being the eternal Son of God, became man, and so was, and continueth to be, God and man in two distinct natures, and one person, forever.

Q. 22. *How did Christ, being the Son of God, become man?*
A. Christ, the Son of God, became man, by taking to himself a true body and a reasonable soul, being conceived by the power of the Holy Ghost in the womb of the virgin Mary, and born of her, yet without sin.

🔊 Ten Commandments: Recite as a Family

And God spake all these words, saying,
I am the Lord thy God, which have brought thee out of the land of Egypt, out of the house of bondage.
1. Thou shalt have no other gods before me.
2. Thou shalt not make unto thee any graven image, or any likeness of any thing that is in heaven above, or that is in the earth beneath, or that is in the water under the earth. Thou shalt not bow down thyself to them, nor serve them: for I the Lord thy God am a jealous God, visiting the iniquity of the fathers upon the children unto the third and fourth generation of them that hate me; And shewing mercy unto thousands of them that love me, and keep my commandments.
3. Thou shalt not take the name of the Lord thy God in vain; for the Lord will not hold him guiltless that taketh his name in vain.
4. Remember the sabbath day, to keep it holy. Six days shalt thou labour, and do all thy work: But the seventh day is the sabbath of the Lord thy God: in it thou shalt not do any work, thou, nor thy son, nor thy daughter, thy manservant, nor thy maidservant, nor thy cattle, nor thy stranger that is within thy gates: For in six days the Lord made heaven and earth, the sea, and all that in them is, and rested the seventh day:

wherefore the Lord blessed the sabbath day, and hallowed it.

5. Honour thy father and thy mother: that thy days may be long upon the land which the Lord thy God giveth thee.
6. Thou shalt not kill.
7. Thou shalt not commit adultery.
8. Thou shalt not steal.
9. Thou shalt not bear false witness against thy neighbour.
10. Thou shalt not covet thy neighbour's house, thou shalt not covet thy neighbour's wife, nor his manservant, nor his maidservant, nor his ox, nor his ass, nor any thing that is thy neighbour's.

✋ Prayer Requests of the Week

Our Family

•

•

•

The Church

•

•

The World

•

•

•

🔊 **The Lord's Prayer: Recite Together**

Our Father which art in heaven, Hallowed be thy name. Thy kingdom come, Thy will be done in earth, as it is in heaven. Give us this day our daily bread. And forgive us our debts, as we forgive our debtors. And lead us not into temptation, but deliver us from evil: For thine is the kingdom, and the power, and the glory, forever. Amen.

🎵 **Optional Singing:** Select a "psalm, hymn, or spiritual song" (Ephesians 5:19), from the Psalter, the church hymnal, or a Youtube worship playlist.

📣 **Exercises For Children**
In the free space on this page: (1) write out one of the catechism questions, (2) practice writing out or spelling some of the key words from the Scripture reading, or (3) draw a picture of something important from today's family discussion.

Family Activity Suggestion: Plant something! A flower, a vegetable, a bush or tree. Make sure to water it! See Appendix #1 for other quality time ideas.

SERMON NOTES ON THIS WEEK'S TEXT

DATE

PREACHER

INTRODUCTION

MAIN IDEAS

PERSONAL or FAMILY APPLICATIONS

🖐 Call to Worship, Psalm 95 KJV
(Traditionally called the Venite Exultemus Domino)

[1] O come, let us sing unto the Lord: let us make a joyful noise to the rock of our salvation. [2] Let us come before his presence with thanksgiving, and make a joyful noise unto him with psalms. [3] For the Lord is a great God, and a great King above all gods. [4] In his hand are the deep places of the earth: the strength of the hills is his also. [5] The sea is his, and he made it: and his hands formed the dry land. [6] O come, let us worship and bow down: let us kneel before the Lord our maker. [7] For he is our God; and we are the people of his pasture, and the sheep of his hand.

📖 Scripture Reading: Mark 4:21-34 (NKJV)

[21] Also He said to them, "Is a lamp brought to be put under a basket or under a bed? Is it not to be set on a lampstand? [22] For there is nothing hidden which will not be revealed, nor has anything been kept secret but that it should come to light. [23] If anyone has ears to hear, let him hear."

[24] Then He said to them, "Take heed what you hear. With the same measure you use, it will be measured to you; and to you who hear, more will be given. [25] For whoever has, to him more will be given; but whoever does not have, even what he has will be taken away from him."

[26] And He said, "The kingdom of God is as if a man should scatter seed on the ground, [27] and should sleep by night and rise by day, and the seed should sprout and grow, he himself does not know how. [28] For the earth yields crops by itself: first the blade, then the head, after that the full grain in the head. [29] But when the grain

ripens, immediately he puts in the sickle, because the harvest has come."

30 Then He said, "To what shall we liken the kingdom of God? Or with what parable shall we picture it? 31 *It is* like a mustard seed which, when it is sown on the ground, is smaller than all the seeds on earth; 32 but when it is sown, it grows up and becomes greater than all herbs, and shoots out large branches, so that the birds of the air may nest under its shade."

33 And with many such parables He spoke the word to them as they were able to hear *it.* 34 But without a parable He did not speak to them. And when they were alone, He explained all things to His disciples.

➡ Scripture Reflection on Today's Reading

Put a circle around difficult words and phrases.

Put a star next to verses that cause us to praise and give thanks.

Underline verses with commands or that lead us to repent.

Put a box around key concepts and other family discussion points.

🎓 Westminster Catechism Questions

Q. 23. *What offices doth Christ execute as our redeemer?*
A. Christ, as our redeemer, executeth the offices of a prophet, of a priest, and of a king, both in his estate of humiliation and exaltation.

Q. 24. *How doth Christ execute the office of a prophet?*
A. Christ executeth the office of a prophet, in revealing to us, by his word and Spirit, the will of God for our salvation.

🔊 Heidelberg Catechism Question #1

Question 1. What is thy only comfort in life and death?

Answer: That I with body and soul, both in life and death, am not my own, but belong unto my faithful Saviour Jesus Christ; who, with his precious blood, has fully satisfied for all my sins, and delivered me from all the power of the devil; and so preserves me that without the will of my heavenly Father, not a hair can fall from my head; yea, that all things must be subservient to my salvation, and therefore, by his Holy Spirit, He also assures me of eternal life, and makes me sincerely willing and ready, henceforth, to live unto him.

🙌 Prayer Requests of the Week

Our Family

-
-
-

The Church

-
-
-

The World

-
-

🔊 The Lord's Prayer: Recite Together

Our Father which art in heaven, Hallowed be thy name. Thy kingdom come, Thy will be done in earth, as it is in heaven. Give us this day our daily bread. And forgive us our debts, as we forgive our debtors. And lead us not into temptation, but deliver us from evil: For thine is the kingdom, and the power, and the glory, forever. Amen.

🎵 **Optional Singing:** Select a "psalm, hymn, or spiritual song" (Ephesians 5:19), from the Psalter, the church hymnal, or a Youtube worship playlist.

➡ Exercises For Children
In the free space on this page: (1) write out one of the catechism questions, (2) practice writing out or spelling some of the key words from the Scripture reading, or (3) draw a picture of something important from today's family discussion.

Family Activity Suggestion: Make a homemade card, or write a special letter to a shut-in from the church or someone who is in need of some special love this week. See Appendix #1 for other quality time ideas.

SERMON NOTES ON THIS WEEK'S TEXT

DATE

PREACHER

INTRODUCTION

MAIN IDEAS

PERSONAL or FAMILY APPLICATIONS

🔥 **Opening Prayer (from the Book of Common Prayer). All pray together, or head of household may lead.**

Almighty God, to whom all hearts are open, all desires known, and from whom no secrets are hid; cleanse the thoughts of our hearts by the inspiration of Thy Holy Spirit, that we may more perfectly love Thee, and more worthily magnify Thy holy name, through Jesus Christ our Lord, Amen.

📖 **Scripture Reading: Mark 4:35-41 (ESV)**

[35] On that day, when evening had come, he said to them, "Let us go across to the other side." [36] And leaving the crowd, they took him with them in the boat, just as he was. And other boats were with him. [37] And a great windstorm arose, and the waves were breaking into the boat, so that the boat was already filling. [38] But he was in the stern, asleep on the cushion. And they woke him and said to him, "Teacher, do you not care that we are perishing?" [39] And he awoke and rebuked the wind and said to the sea, "Peace! Be still!" And the wind ceased, and there was a great calm. [40] He said to them, "Why are you so afraid? Have you still no faith?" [41] And they were filled with great fear and said to one another, "Who then is this, that even the wind and the sea obey him?"

↦ **Scripture Reflection on Today's Reading**

Put a circle around difficult words and phrases.

Put a star next to verses that cause us to praise and give thanks.

Underline verses with commands or that lead us to repent.

Put a box around key concepts and other family discussion points.

🎓 Westminster Catechism Questions

Q. 25. *How doth Christ execute the office of a priest?*
A. Christ executeth the office of a priest, in his once offering up of himself a sacrifice to satisfy divine justice, and reconcile us to God; and in making continual intercession for us.

Q. 26. *How doth Christ execute the office of a king?*
A. Christ executeth the office of a king, in subduing us to himself, in ruling and defending us, and in restraining and conquering all his and our enemies.

🔊 Apostle's Creed: Recite as a Family

I believe in God the Father Almighty, Maker of heaven and earth. I believe in Jesus Christ, His only Son, our Lord, who was conceived by the Holy Spirit, and born of the Virgin Mary. He suffered under Pontius Pilate, was crucified, died, and was buried; he descended into hell. The third day he rose again from the dead. He ascended into heaven, he is seated at the right hand of God the Father Almighty. From there he will come to judge the living and the dead. I believe in the Holy Spirit, the holy catholic church, the communion of saints, the forgiveness of sins, the resurrection of the body, and the life everlasting. Amen.

✋ Prayer Requests of the Week

Our Family

-

-

●

The Church

●

●

●

●

The World

●

●

●

🔊 **The Lord's Prayer: Recite Together**

Our Father which art in heaven, Hallowed be thy name. Thy kingdom come, Thy will be done in earth, as it is in heaven. Give us this day our daily bread. And forgive us our debts, as we forgive our debtors. And lead us not into temptation, but deliver us from evil: For thine is the kingdom, and the power, and the glory, forever. Amen.

🎵 **Optional Singing:** Select a "psalm, hymn, or spiritual song" (Ephesians 5:19), from the Psalter, the church hymnal, or a Youtube worship playlist.

✏ Exercises For Children

In the free space on this page: (1) write out one of the catechism questions, (2) practice writing out or spelling some of the key words from the Scripture reading, or (3) draw a picture of something important from today's family discussion.

Family Activity Suggestion: Write a letter to a solider from your congregation. If possible, send a care package of their favorite snacks. See Appendix #1 for other quality time ideas.

SERMON NOTES ON THIS WEEK'S TEXT

DATE

PREACHER

INTRODUCTION

MAIN IDEAS

PERSONAL or FAMILY APPLICATIONS

👆 Opening Prayer (from the Book of Common Prayer). All pray together, or head of household may lead.

Almighty God, to whom all hearts are open, all desires known, and from whom no secrets are hid; cleanse the thoughts of our hearts by the inspiration of Thy Holy Spirit, that we may more perfectly love Thee, and more worthily magnify Thy holy name, through Jesus Christ our Lord, Amen.

📖 Scripture Reading: Mark 5:1-20 (ESV)

They came to the other side of the sea, to the country of the Gerasenes. [2] And when Jesus had stepped out of the boat, immediately there met him out of the tombs a man with an unclean spirit. [3] He lived among the tombs. And no one could bind him anymore, not even with a chain, [4] for he had often been bound with shackles and chains, but he wrenched the chains apart, and he broke the shackles in pieces. No one had the strength to subdue him. [5] Night and day among the tombs and on the mountains he was always crying out and cutting himself with stones. [6] And when he saw Jesus from afar, he ran and fell down before him. [7] And crying out with a loud voice, he said, "What have you to do with me, Jesus, Son of the Most High God? I adjure you by God, do not torment me." [8] For he was saying to him, "Come out of the man, you unclean spirit!" [9] And Jesus asked him, "What is your name?" He replied, "My name is Legion, for we are many." [10] And he begged him earnestly not to send them out of the country. [11] Now a great herd of pigs was feeding there on the hillside, [12] and they begged him, saying, "Send us to the pigs; let us enter them." [13] So he gave them permission. And the unclean spirits came out and entered the pigs; and the herd, numbering about two thousand, rushed down the steep bank into the sea and drowned in the sea.

14 The herdsmen fled and told it in the city and in the country. And people came to see what it was that had happened. **15** And they came to Jesus and saw the demon-possessed man, the one who had had the legion, sitting there, clothed and in his right mind, and they were afraid. **16** And those who had seen it described to them what had happened to the demon-possessed man and to the pigs. **17** And they began to beg Jesus to depart from their region. **18** As he was getting into the boat, the man who had been possessed with demons begged him that he might be with him. **19** And he did not permit him but said to him, "Go home to your friends and tell them how much the Lord has done for you, and how he has had mercy on you."**20** And he went away and began to proclaim in the Decapolis how much Jesus had done for him, and everyone marveled.

➖ Scripture Reflection on Today's Reading

Put a circle around difficult words and phrases.

Put a star next to verses that cause us to praise and give thanks.

Underline verses with commands or that lead us to repent.

Put a box around key concepts and other family discussion points.

🎓 Westminster Catechism Questions

Q. 27. *Wherein did Christ's humiliation consist?*
A. Christ's humiliation consisted in his being born, and that in a low condition, made under the law, undergoing the miseries of this life, the wrath of God, and the cursed death of the cross; in being buried, and continuing under the power of death for a time.

Q. 28. *Wherein consisteth Christ's exaltation?*

A. Christ's exaltation consisteth in his rising again from the dead on the third day, in ascending up into heaven, in sitting at the right hand of God the Father, and in coming to judge the world at the last day.

🔊 Nicene Creed: Recite as a Family

We believe in one God, the Father Almighty, Maker of heaven and earth, and of all things visible and invisible.
And in one Lord Jesus Christ, the only-begotten Son of God, begotten of the Father before all worlds; God of God, Light of Light, very God of very God; begotten, not made, being of one substance with the Father, by whom all things were made. Who, for us and for our salvation, came down from heaven, and was incarnate by the Holy Spirit of the virgin Mary, and was made man; and was crucified also for us under Pontius Pilate; He suffered and was buried; and the third day He rose again, according to the Scriptures; and ascended into heaven, and sits on the right hand of the Father; and He shall come again, with glory, to judge the living and the dead; whose kingdom shall have no end.
And we believe in the Holy Ghost, the Lord and Giver of Life, who proceeds from the Father and the Son; who with the Father and the Son together is worshipped and glorified; who spoke by the prophets. And we believe in one holy catholic and apostolic Church. We acknowledge one baptism for the remission of sins; and we look for the resurrection of the dead, and the life of the world to come. Amen.

✋ Prayer Requests of the Week

Our Family

-

-

-

The Church

-

-

-

The World

-

-

-

🔊 The Lord's Prayer: Recite Together

Our Father which art in heaven, Hallowed be thy name. Thy kingdom come, Thy will be done in earth, as it is in heaven. Give us this day our daily bread. And forgive us our debts, as we forgive our debtors. And lead us not into temptation, but deliver us from evil: For thine is the kingdom, and the power, and the glory, forever. Amen.

🎵 **Optional Singing:** Select a "psalm, hymn, or spiritual song" (Ephesians 5:19), from the Psalter, the church hymnal, or a Youtube worship playlist.

✏ Exercises For Children

In the free space on this page: (1) write out one of the catechism questions, (2) practice writing out or spelling some of the key words from the Scripture reading, or (3) draw a picture of something important from today's family discussion.

Family Activity Suggestion: Make some baked goods to share with neighbors. Bring a leaflet about our church, and invite them to attend with you this coming Sunday. See Appendix #1 for other quality time ideas.

SERMON NOTES ON THIS WEEK'S TEXT

DATE

PREACHER

INTRODUCTION

MAIN IDEAS

PERSONAL or FAMILY APPLICATIONS

✋ **Opening Prayer (from the Book of Common Prayer). All pray together, or head of household may lead.**

Almighty God, to whom all hearts are open, all desires known, and from whom no secrets are hid; cleanse the thoughts of our hearts by the inspiration of Thy Holy Spirit, that we may more perfectly love Thee, and more worthily magnify Thy holy name, through Jesus Christ our Lord, Amen.

📖 **Scripture Reading: Mark 5:21-43 (NKJV)**

[21] Now when Jesus had crossed over again by boat to the other side, a great multitude gathered to Him; and He was by the sea. [22] And behold, one of the rulers of the synagogue came, Jairus by name. And when he saw Him, he fell at His feet [23] and begged Him earnestly, saying, "My little daughter lies at the point of death. Come and lay Your hands on her, that she may be healed, and she will live." [24] So *Jesus* went with him, and a great multitude followed Him and thronged Him.
[25] Now a certain woman had a flow of blood for twelve years, [26] and had suffered many things from many physicians. She had spent all that she had and was no better, but rather grew worse. [27] When she heard about Jesus, she came behind *Him* in the crowd and touched His garment. [28] For she said, "If only I may touch His clothes, I shall be made well."
[29] Immediately the fountain of her blood was dried up, and she felt in *her* body that she was healed of the affliction. [30] And Jesus, immediately knowing in Himself that power had gone out of Him, turned around in the crowd and said, "Who touched My clothes?"
[31] But His disciples said to Him, "You see the multitude thronging You, and You say, 'Who touched Me?' "

[32] And He looked around to see her who had done this thing. [33] But the woman, fearing and trembling, knowing what had happened to her, came and fell down before Him and told Him the whole truth. [34] And He said to her, "Daughter, your faith has made you well. Go in peace, and be healed of your affliction."

[35] While He was still speaking, *some* came from the ruler of the synagogue's *house* who said, "Your daughter is dead. Why trouble the Teacher any further?"

[36] As soon as Jesus heard the word that was spoken, He said to the ruler of the synagogue, "Do not be afraid; only believe." [37] And He permitted no one to follow Him except Peter, James, and John the brother of James. [38] Then He came to the house of the ruler of the synagogue, and saw a tumult and those who wept and wailed loudly. [39] When He came in, He said to them, "Why make this commotion and weep? The child is not dead, but sleeping."

[40] And they ridiculed Him. But when He had put them all outside, He took the father and the mother of the child, and those *who were* with Him, and entered where the child was lying. [41] Then He took the child by the hand, and said to her, "Talitha, cumi," which is translated, "Little girl, I say to you, arise." [42] Immediately the girl arose and walked, for she was twelve years *of age*. And they were overcome with great amazement. [43] But He commanded them strictly that no one should know it, and said that *something* should be given her to eat.

➤ Scripture Reflection on Today's Reading

Put a circle around difficult words and phrases.

Put a star next to verses that cause us to praise and give thanks.

Underline verses with commands or that lead us to repent.

Put a box around key concepts and other family discussion points.

♕ Westminster Catechism Questions

Q. 29. *How are we made partakers of the redemption purchased by Christ?*
A. We are made partakers of the redemption purchased by Christ, by the effectual application of it to us by his Holy Spirit.

Q. 30. *How doth the Spirit apply to us the redemption purchased by Christ?*
A. The Spirit applieth to us the redemption purchased by Christ, by working faith in us, and thereby uniting us to Christ in our effectual calling.

◀》 Ten Commandments: Recite as a Family

And God spake all these words, saying,
I am the Lord thy God, which have brought thee out of the land of Egypt, out of the house of bondage.

1. Thou shalt have no other gods before me.
2. Thou shalt not make unto thee any graven image, or any likeness of any thing that is in heaven above, or that is in the earth beneath, or that is in the water under the earth. Thou shalt not bow down thyself to them, nor serve them: for I the Lord thy God am a jealous God, visiting the iniquity of the fathers upon the children unto the third and fourth generation of them that hate me; And shewing mercy unto thousands of them that love me, and keep my commandments.
3. Thou shalt not take the name of the Lord thy God in vain; for the Lord will not hold him guiltless that taketh his name in vain.
4. Remember the sabbath day, to keep it holy. Six days shalt thou labour, and do all thy work: But the seventh day is the sabbath of the Lord thy God: in it thou shalt not do any work, thou, nor thy son, nor thy daughter, thy manservant, nor thy

maidservant, nor thy cattle, nor thy stranger that is within thy gates: For in six days the Lord made heaven and earth, the sea, and all that in them is, and rested the seventh day: wherefore the Lord blessed the sabbath day, and hallowed it.

5. Honour thy father and thy mother: that thy days may be long upon the land which the Lord thy God giveth thee.
6. Thou shalt not kill.
7. Thou shalt not commit adultery.
8. Thou shalt not steal.
9. Thou shalt not bear false witness against thy neighbour.
10. Thou shalt not covet thy neighbour's house, thou shalt not covet thy neighbour's wife, nor his manservant, nor his maidservant, nor his ox, nor his ass, nor any thing that is thy neighbour's.

✋ Prayer Requests of the Week

Our Family

•

•

The Church

•

•

The World

•

-

◄)) The Lord's Prayer: Recite Together

Our Father which art in heaven, Hallowed be thy name. Thy kingdom come, Thy will be done in earth, as it is in heaven. Give us this day our daily bread. And forgive us our debts, as we forgive our debtors. And lead us not into temptation, but deliver us from evil: For thine is the kingdom, and the power, and the glory, forever. Amen.

♪♪ Optional Singing: Select a "psalm, hymn, or spiritual song" (Ephesians 5:19), from the Psalter, the church hymnal, or a Youtube worship playlist.

•— Exercises For Children
In the free space on this page: (1) write out one of the catechism questions, (2) practice writing out or spelling some of the key words from the Scripture reading, or (3) draw a picture of something important from today's family discussion.

Family Activity Suggestion: Play a simple game of family charades. Boys versus girls! Each person should write some items to act out and put them in a bowl. See Appendix #1 for other quality time ideas.

SERMON NOTES ON THIS WEEK'S TEXT

DATE

PREACHER

INTRODUCTION

MAIN IDEAS

PERSONAL or FAMILY APPLICATIONS

👆 Call to Worship, Psalm 95 KJV
(Traditionally called the Venite Exultemus Domino)

[1] O come, let us sing unto the Lord: let us make a joyful noise to the rock of our salvation. [2] Let us come before his presence with thanksgiving, and make a joyful noise unto him with psalms. [3] For the Lord is a great God, and a great King above all gods. [4] In his hand are the deep places of the earth: the strength of the hills is his also. [5] The sea is his, and he made it: and his hands formed the dry land. [6] O come, let us worship and bow down: let us kneel before the Lord our maker. [7] For he is our God; and we are the people of his pasture, and the sheep of his hand.

📖 Scripture Reading: Mark 6:1-13 (ESV)

He went away from there and came to his hometown, and his disciples followed him. [2] And on the Sabbath he began to teach in the synagogue, and many who heard him were astonished, saying, "Where did this man get these things? What is the wisdom given to him? How are such mighty works done by his hands? [3] Is not this the carpenter, the son of Mary and brother of James and Joses and Judas and Simon? And are not his sisters here with us?" And they took offense at him. [4] And Jesus said to them, "A prophet is not without honor, except in his hometown and among his relatives and in his own household." [5] And he could do no mighty work there, except that he laid his hands on a few sick people and healed them. [6] And he marveled because of their unbelief. And he went about among the villages teaching.

[7] And he called the twelve and began to send them out two by two, and gave them authority over the unclean spirits. [8] He charged them to take nothing for their journey except a staff—no bread, no

bag, no money in their belts— [9] but to wear sandals and not put on two tunics. [10] And he said to them, "Whenever you enter a house, stay there until you depart from there. [11] And if any place will not receive you and they will not listen to you, when you leave, shake off the dust that is on your feet as a testimony against them."[12] So they went out and proclaimed that people should repent. [13] And they cast out many demons and anointed with oil many who were sick and healed them.

➡ Scripture Reflection on Today's Reading

Put a circle around difficult words and phrases.

Put a star next to verses that cause us to praise and give thanks.

Underline verses with commands or that lead us to repent.

Put a box around key concepts and other family discussion points.

🎓 Westminster Catechism Questions

Q. 31. *What is effectual calling?*
A. Effectual calling is the work of God's Spirit, whereby, convincing us of our sin and misery, enlightening our minds in the knowledge of Christ, and renewing our wills, he doth persuade and enable us to embrace Jesus Christ, freely offered to us in the gospel.

Q. 32. *What benefits do they that are effectually called partake of in this life?*
A. They that are effectually called do in this life partake of justification, adoption and sanctification, and the several benefits which in this life do either accompany or flow from them.

🔊 Heidelberg Catechism Question #1

Question 1. What is thy only comfort in life and death?

Answer: That I with body and soul, both in life and death, am not my own, but belong unto my faithful Saviour Jesus Christ; who, with his precious blood, has fully satisfied for all my sins, and delivered me from all the power of the devil; and so preserves me that without the will of my heavenly Father, not a hair can fall from my head; yea, that all things must be subservient to my salvation, and therefore, by his Holy Spirit, He also assures me of eternal life, and makes me sincerely willing and ready, henceforth, to live unto him.

✋ Prayer Requests of the Week

Our Family

-
-
-

The Church

-
-
-

The World

-

•

◀)) The Lord's Prayer: Recite Together

Our Father which art in heaven, Hallowed be thy name. Thy kingdom come, Thy will be done in earth, as it is in heaven. Give us this day our daily bread. And forgive us our debts, as we forgive our debtors. And lead us not into temptation, but deliver us from evil: For thine is the kingdom, and the power, and the glory, forever. Amen.

♪♪ **Optional Singing:** Select a "psalm, hymn, or spiritual song" (Ephesians 5:19), from the Psalter, the church hymnal, or a Youtube worship playlist.

▬ Exercises For Children

In the free space on this page: (1) write out one of the catechism questions, (2) practice writing out or spelling some of the key words from the Scripture reading, or (3) draw a picture of something important from today's family discussion.

Family Activity Suggestion: Play spoons. (Card game). No gambling of course! See Appendix #1 for other quality time ideas.

SERMON NOTES ON THIS WEEK'S TEXT

DATE

PREACHER

INTRODUCTION

MAIN IDEAS

PERSONAL or FAMILY APPLICATIONS

🔥 **Opening Prayer (from the Book of Common Prayer). All pray together, or head of household may lead.**

Almighty God, to whom all hearts are open, all desires known, and from whom no secrets are hid; cleanse the thoughts of our hearts by the inspiration of Thy Holy Spirit, that we may more perfectly love Thee, and more worthily magnify Thy holy name, through Jesus Christ our Lord, Amen.

📖 **Scripture Reading: Mark 6:14-29 (ESV)**

14 King Herod heard of it, for Jesus' name had become known. Some said, "John the Baptist has been raised from the dead. That is why these miraculous powers are at work in him." 15 But others said, "He is Elijah." And others said, "He is a prophet, like one of the prophets of old." 16 But when Herod heard of it, he said, "John, whom I beheaded, has been raised." 17 For it was Herod who had sent and seized John and bound him in prison for the sake of Herodias, his brother Philip's wife, because he had married her. 18 For John had been saying to Herod, "It is not lawful for you to have your brother's wife." 19 And Herodias had a grudge against him and wanted to put him to death. But she could not, 20 for Herod feared John, knowing that he was a righteous and holy man, and he kept him safe. When he heard him, he was greatly perplexed, and yet he heard him gladly.

21 But an opportunity came when Herod on his birthday gave a banquet for his nobles and military commanders and the leading men of Galilee. 22 For when Herodias's daughter came in and danced, she pleased Herod and his guests. And the king said to the girl, "Ask me for whatever you wish, and I will give it to you." 23 And he vowed to her, "Whatever you ask me, I will give you, up to half of

my kingdom." [24] And she went out and said to her mother, "For what should I ask?" And she said, "The head of John the Baptist." [25] And she came in immediately with haste to the king and asked, saying, "I want you to give me at once the head of John the Baptist on a platter." [26] And the king was exceedingly sorry, but because of his oaths and his guests he did not want to break his word to her. [27] And immediately the king sent an executioner with orders to bring John's head. He went and beheaded him in the prison [28] and brought his head on a platter and gave it to the girl, and the girl gave it to her mother. [29] When his disciples heard of it, they came and took his body and laid it in a tomb.

▬ Scripture Reflection on Today's Reading

Put a circle around difficult words and phrases.

Put a star next to verses that cause us to praise and give thanks.

Underline verses with commands or that lead us to repent.

Put a box around key concepts and other family discussion points.

🎓 Westminster Catechism Questions

Q. 33. *What is justification?*
A. Justification is an act of God's free grace, wherein he pardoneth all our sins, and accepteth us as righteous in his sight, only for the righteousness of Christ imputed to us, and received by faith alone.

Q. 34. *What is adoption?*
A. Adoption is an act of God's free grace, whereby we are received into the number, and have a right to all the privileges of, the sons of God.

🔊 Apostle's Creed: Recite as a Family

I believe in God the Father Almighty, Maker of heaven and earth. I believe in Jesus Christ, His only Son, our Lord, who was conceived by the Holy Spirit, and born of the Virgin Mary. He suffered under Pontius Pilate, was crucified, died, and was buried; he descended into hell. The third day he rose again from the dead. He ascended into heaven, he is seated at the right hand of God the Father Almighty. From there he will come to judge the living and the dead. I believe in the Holy Spirit, the holy catholic church, the communion of saints, the forgiveness of sins, the resurrection of the body, and the life everlasting. Amen.

✋ Prayer Requests of the Week

Our Family

-

-

-

The Church

-

-

-

The World

-

●

🔊 The Lord's Prayer: Recite Together

Our Father which art in heaven, Hallowed be thy name. Thy kingdom come, Thy will be done in earth, as it is in heaven. Give us this day our daily bread. And forgive us our debts, as we forgive our debtors. And lead us not into temptation, but deliver us from evil: For thine is the kingdom, and the power, and the glory, forever. Amen.

🎵 **Optional Singing:** Select a "psalm, hymn, or spiritual song" (Ephesians 5:19), from the Psalter, the church hymnal, or a Youtube worship playlist.

📢 Exercises For Children

In the free space on this page: (1) write out one of the catechism questions, (2) practice writing out or spelling some of the key words from the Scripture reading, or (3) draw a picture of something important from today's family discussion.

Family Activity Suggestion: Take a walk in the neighborhood park. See Appendix #1 for other quality time ideas.

SERMON NOTES ON THIS WEEK'S TEXT

DATE

PREACHER

INTRODUCTION

MAIN IDEAS

PERSONAL or FAMILY APPLICATIONS

🕯 Opening Prayer (from the Book of Common Prayer). All pray together, or head of household may lead.

Almighty God, to whom all hearts are open, all desires known, and from whom no secrets are hid; cleanse the thoughts of our hearts by the inspiration of Thy Holy Spirit, that we may more perfectly love Thee, and more worthily magnify Thy holy name, through Jesus Christ our Lord, Amen.

📖 Scripture Reading: Mark 6:30-44 (ESV)

[30] The apostles returned to Jesus and told him all that they had done and taught. [31] And he said to them, "Come away by yourselves to a desolate place and rest a while." For many were coming and going, and they had no leisure even to eat. [32] And they went away in the boat to a desolate place by themselves. [33] Now many saw them going and recognized them, and they ran there on foot from all the towns and got there ahead of them. [34] When he went ashore he saw a great crowd, and he had compassion on them, because they were like sheep without a shepherd. And he began to teach them many things. [35] And when it grew late, his disciples came to him and said, "This is a desolate place, and the hour is now late. [36] Send them away to go into the surrounding countryside and villages and buy themselves something to eat." [37] But he answered them, "You give them something to eat." And they said to him, "Shall we go and buy two hundred denarii worth of bread and give it to them to eat?" [38] And he said to them, "How many loaves do you have? Go and see." And when they had found out, they said, "Five, and two fish." [39] Then he commanded them all to sit down in groups on the green grass. [40] So they sat down in groups, by hundreds and by fifties. [41] And taking the five loaves and the two fish, he looked up to heaven and said a blessing and broke the

loaves and gave them to the disciples to set before the people. And he divided the two fish among them all. [42] And they all ate and were satisfied. [43] And they took up twelve baskets full of broken pieces and of the fish.[44] And those who ate the loaves were five thousand men.

➡ Scripture Reflection on Today's Reading

Put a circle around difficult words and phrases.

Put a star next to verses that cause us to praise and give thanks.

Underline verses with commands or that lead us to repent.

Put a box around key concepts and other family discussion points.

Westminster Catechism Questions

Q. 35. *What is sanctification?*
A. Sanctification is the work of God's free grace, whereby we are renewed in the whole man after the image of God, and are enabled more and more to die unto sin, and live unto righteousness.

Q. 36. *What are the benefits which in this life do accompany or flow from justification, adoption and sanctification?*
A. The benefits which in this life do accompany or flow from justification, adoption and sanctification, are, assurance of God's love, peace of conscience, joy in the Holy Ghost, increase of grace, and perseverance therein to the end.

◀》 Nicene Creed: Recite as a Family

We believe in one God, the Father Almighty, Maker of heaven and earth, and of all things visible and invisible.

And in one Lord Jesus Christ, the only-begotten Son of God, begotten of the Father before all worlds; God of God, Light of Light, very God of very God; begotten, not made, being of one substance with the Father, by whom all things were made. Who, for us and for our salvation, came down from heaven, and was incarnate by the Holy Spirit of the virgin Mary, and was made man; and was crucified also for us under Pontius Pilate; He suffered and was buried; and the third day He rose again, according to the Scriptures; and ascended into heaven, and sits on the right hand of the Father; and He shall come again, with glory, to judge the living and the dead; whose kingdom shall have no end.
And we believe in the Holy Ghost, the Lord and Giver of Life, who proceeds from the Father and the Son; who with the Father and the Son together is worshipped and glorified; who spoke by the prophets. And we believe in one holy catholic and apostolic Church. We acknowledge one baptism for the remission of sins; and we look for the resurrection of the dead, and the life of the world to come. Amen.

✋ Prayer Requests of the Week

Our Family

-
-
-

The Church

-
-

The World

-

-

🔊 **The Lord's Prayer: Recite Together**

Our Father which art in heaven, Hallowed be thy name. Thy kingdom come, Thy will be done in earth, as it is in heaven. Give us this day our daily bread. And forgive us our debts, as we forgive our debtors. And lead us not into temptation, but deliver us from evil: For thine is the kingdom, and the power, and the glory, forever. Amen.

🎵 **Optional Singing:** Select a "psalm, hymn, or spiritual song" (Ephesians 5:19), from the Psalter, the church hymnal, or a Youtube worship playlist.

👉 **Exercises For Children**
In the free space on this page: (1) write out one of the catechism questions, (2) practice writing out or spelling some of the key words from the Scripture reading, or (3) draw a picture of something important from today's family discussion.

Family Activity Suggestion: Buy or create a bird or squirrel feeder. If possible, place it in view of a nearby window. See Appendix #1 for other quality time ideas.

SERMON NOTES ON THIS WEEK'S TEXT

DATE

PREACHER

INTRODUCTION

MAIN IDEAS

PERSONAL or FAMILY APPLICATIONS

🖐 **Opening Prayer (from the Book of Common Prayer). All pray together, or head of household may lead.**

Almighty God, to whom all hearts are open, all desires known, and from whom no secrets are hid; cleanse the thoughts of our hearts by the inspiration of Thy Holy Spirit, that we may more perfectly love Thee, and more worthily magnify Thy holy name, through Jesus Christ our Lord, Amen.

📖 **Scripture Reading: Mark 6:45-56 (ESV)**

[45] Immediately he made his disciples get into the boat and go before him to the other side, to Bethsaida, while he dismissed the crowd. [46] And after he had taken leave of them, he went up on the mountain to pray. [47] And when evening came, the boat was out on the sea, and he was alone on the land. [48] And he saw that they were making headway painfully, for the wind was against them. And about the fourth watch of the night he came to them, walking on the sea. He meant to pass by them, [49] but when they saw him walking on the sea they thought it was a ghost, and cried out, [50] for they all saw him and were terrified. But immediately he spoke to them and said, "Take heart; it is I. Do not be afraid."[51] And he got into the boat with them, and the wind ceased. And they were utterly astounded, [52] for they did not understand about the loaves, but their hearts were hardened.

[53] When they had crossed over, they came to land at Gennesaret and moored to the shore. [54] And when they got out of the boat, the people immediately recognized him [55] and ran about the whole region and began to bring the sick people on their beds to wherever they heard he was. [56] And wherever he came, in villages, cities, or countryside, they laid the sick in the marketplaces and implored him

that they might touch even the fringe of his garment. And as many as touched it were made well.

➥ Scripture Reflection on Today's Reading

Put a circle around difficult words and phrases.

Put a star next to verses that cause us to praise and give thanks.

Underline verses with commands or that lead us to repent.

Put a box around key concepts and other family discussion points.

✒ Westminster Catechism Questions

Q. 37. *What benefits do believers receive from Christ at death?*
A. The souls of believers are at their death made perfect in holiness, and do immediately pass into glory; and their bodies, being still united to Christ, do rest in their graves till the resurrection.

Q. 38. *What benefits do believers receive from Christ at the resurrection?*
A. At the resurrection, believers being raised up in glory, shall be openly acknowledged and acquitted in the day of judgment, and made perfectly blessed in the full enjoying of God to all eternity.

◀» Ten Commandments: Recite as a Family

And God spake all these words, saying,
I am the Lord thy God, which have brought thee out of the land of Egypt, out of the house of bondage.
   1. Thou shalt have no other gods before me.

2. Thou shalt not make unto thee any graven image, or any likeness of any thing that is in heaven above, or that is in the earth beneath, or that is in the water under the earth. Thou shalt not bow down thyself to them, nor serve them: for I the Lord thy God am a jealous God, visiting the iniquity of the fathers upon the children unto the third and fourth generation of them that hate me; And shewing mercy unto thousands of them that love me, and keep my commandments.
3. Thou shalt not take the name of the Lord thy God in vain; for the Lord will not hold him guiltless that taketh his name in vain.
4. Remember the sabbath day, to keep it holy. Six days shalt thou labour, and do all thy work: But the seventh day is the sabbath of the Lord thy God: in it thou shalt not do any work, thou, nor thy son, nor thy daughter, thy manservant, nor thy maidservant, nor thy cattle, nor thy stranger that is within thy gates: For in six days the Lord made heaven and earth, the sea, and all that in them is, and rested the seventh day: wherefore the Lord blessed the sabbath day, and hallowed it.
5. Honour thy father and thy mother: that thy days may be long upon the land which the Lord thy God giveth thee.
6. Thou shalt not kill.
7. Thou shalt not commit adultery.
8. Thou shalt not steal.
9. Thou shalt not bear false witness against thy neighbour.
10. Thou shalt not covet thy neighbour's house, thou shalt not covet thy neighbour's wife, nor his manservant, nor his maidservant, nor his ox, nor his ass, nor any thing that is thy neighbour's.

🖐 Prayer Requests of the Week

Our Family

-
-
-

The Church

-
-
-

The World

-
-
-

🔊 **The Lord's Prayer: Recite Together**

Our Father which art in heaven, Hallowed be thy name. Thy kingdom come, Thy will be done in earth, as it is in heaven. Give us this day our daily bread. And forgive us our debts, as we forgive our debtors. And lead us not into temptation, but deliver us from evil: For thine is the kingdom, and the power, and the glory, forever. Amen.

♪♪ **Optional Singing:** Select a "psalm, hymn, or spiritual song" (Ephesians 5:19), from the Psalter, the church hymnal, or a Youtube worship playlist.

➡ Exercises For Children

In the free space on this page: (1) write out one of the catechism questions, (2) practice writing out or spelling some of the key words from the Scripture reading, or (3) draw a picture of something important from today's family discussion.

Family Activity Suggestion: Attempt some simple star gazing in the evening. Phone apps or astronomy books can help you identify the constellations. See Appendix #1 for other quality time ideas.

SERMON NOTES ON THIS WEEK'S TEXT

DATE

PREACHER

INTRODUCTION

MAIN IDEAS

PERSONAL or FAMILY APPLICATIONS

🔥 Call to Worship, Psalm 95 KJV
(Traditionally called the Venite Exultemus Domino)

[1] O come, let us sing unto the Lord: let us make a joyful noise to the rock of our salvation. [2] Let us come before his presence with thanksgiving, and make a joyful noise unto him with psalms. [3] For the Lord is a great God, and a great King above all gods. [4] In his hand are the deep places of the earth: the strength of the hills is his also. [5] The sea is his, and he made it: and his hands formed the dry land. [6] O come, let us worship and bow down: let us kneel before the Lord our maker. [7] For he is our God; and we are the people of his pasture, and the sheep of his hand.

📖 Scripture Reading: Mark 7:1-13 (ESV)

Now when the Pharisees gathered to him, with some of the scribes who had come from Jerusalem, [2] they saw that some of his disciples ate with hands that were defiled, that is, unwashed. [3] (For the Pharisees and all the Jews do not eat unless they wash their hands properly, holding to the tradition of the elders, [4] and when they come from the marketplace, they do not eat unless they wash. And there are many other traditions that they observe, such as the washing of cups and pots and copper vessels and dining couches.) [5] And the Pharisees and the scribes asked him, "Why do your disciples not walk according to the tradition of the elders, but eat with defiled hands?" [6] And he said to them, "Well did Isaiah prophesy of you hypocrites, as it is written,
"'This people honors me with their lips,
    but their heart is far from me;
[7] in vain do they worship me,
    teaching as doctrines the commandments of men.'

⁸ You leave the commandment of God and hold to the tradition of men."

⁹ And he said to them, "You have a fine way of rejecting the commandment of God in order to establish your tradition!¹⁰ For Moses said, 'Honor your father and your mother'; and, 'Whoever reviles father or mother must surely die.' ¹¹ But you say, 'If a man tells his father or his mother, "Whatever you would have gained from me is Corban"' (that is, given to God)— ¹² then you no longer permit him to do anything for his father or mother, ¹³ thus making void the word of God by your tradition that you have handed down. And many such things you do."

← Scripture Reflection on Today's Reading

Put a circle around difficult words and phrases.

Put a star next to verses that cause us to praise and give thanks.

Underline verses with commands or that lead us to repent.

Put a box around key concepts and other family discussion points.

🎓 Westminster Catechism Questions

Q. 39. *What is the duty which God requireth of man?*
A. The duty which God requireth of man is obedience to his revealed will.

Q. 40. *What did God at first reveal to man for the rule of his obedience?*
A. The rule which God at first revealed to man for his obedience was the moral law.

🔊 Heidelberg Catechism Question #1

Question 1. What is thy only comfort in life and death?

Answer: That I with body and soul, both in life and death, am not my own, but belong unto my faithful Saviour Jesus Christ; who, with his precious blood, has fully satisfied for all my sins, and delivered me from all the power of the devil; and so preserves me that without the will of my heavenly Father, not a hair can fall from my head; yea, that all things must be subservient to my salvation, and therefore, by his Holy Spirit, He also assures me of eternal life, and makes me sincerely willing and ready, henceforth, to live unto him.

🖐 Prayer Requests of the Week

Our Family

-

-

-

The Church

-

-

-

The World

-

●

🔊 The Lord's Prayer: Recite Together

Our Father which art in heaven, Hallowed be thy name. Thy kingdom come, Thy will be done in earth, as it is in heaven. Give us this day our daily bread. And forgive us our debts, as we forgive our debtors. And lead us not into temptation, but deliver us from evil: For thine is the kingdom, and the power, and the glory, forever. Amen.

🎵 **Optional Singing:** Select a "psalm, hymn, or spiritual song" (Ephesians 5:19), from the Psalter, the church hymnal, or a Youtube worship playlist.

▬ Exercises For Children
In the free space on this page: (1) write out one of the catechism questions, (2) practice writing out or spelling some of the key words from the Scripture reading, or (3) draw a picture of something important from today's family discussion.

Family Activity Suggestion: Take a bike ride around the neighborhood! See Appendix #1 for other quality time ideas.

SERMON NOTES ON THIS WEEK'S TEXT

DATE

PREACHER

INTRODUCTION

MAIN IDEAS

PERSONAL or FAMILY APPLICATIONS

✋ Opening Prayer (from the Book of Common Prayer). All pray together, or head of household may lead.

Almighty God, to whom all hearts are open, all desires known, and from whom no secrets are hid; cleanse the thoughts of our hearts by the inspiration of Thy Holy Spirit, that we may more perfectly love Thee, and more worthily magnify Thy holy name, through Jesus Christ our Lord, Amen.

📖 Scripture Reading: Mark 7:14-23 (NKJV)

[14] When He had called all the multitude to *Himself,* He said to them, "Hear Me, everyone, and understand: [15] There is nothing that enters a man from outside which can defile him; but the things which come out of him, those are the things that defile a man. [16] If anyone has ears to hear, let him hear!" [17] When He had entered a house away from the crowd, His disciples asked Him concerning the parable. [18] So He said to them, "Are you thus without understanding also? Do you not perceive that whatever enters a man from outside cannot defile him, [19] because it does not enter his heart but his stomach, and is eliminated, *thus* purifying all foods?"[20] And He said, "What comes out of a man, that defiles a man. [21] For from within, out of the heart of men, proceed evil thoughts, adulteries, fornications, murders, [22] thefts, covetousness, wickedness, deceit, lewdness, an evil eye, blasphemy, pride, foolishness. [23] All these evil things come from within and defile a man."

👄 Scripture Reflection on Today's Reading

Put a circle around difficult words and phrases.

Put a star next to verses that cause us to praise and give thanks.

Underline verses with commands or that lead us to repent.

Put a box around key concepts and other family discussion points.

🎓 Westminster Catechism Questions

Q. 41. *Where is the moral law summarily comprehended?*
A. The moral law is summarily comprehended in the ten commandments.

Q. 42. *What is the sum of the ten commandments?*
A. The sum of the ten commandments is to love the Lord our God with all our heart, with all our soul, with all our strength, and with all our mind; and our neighbor as ourselves.

🔊 Apostle's Creed: Recite as a Family

I believe in God the Father Almighty, Maker of heaven and earth. I believe in Jesus Christ, His only Son, our Lord, who was conceived by the Holy Spirit, and born of the Virgin Mary. He suffered under Pontius Pilate, was crucified, died, and was buried; he descended into hell. The third day he rose again from the dead. He ascended into heaven, he is seated at the right hand of God the Father Almighty. From there he will come to judge the living and the dead. I believe in the Holy Spirit, the holy catholic church, the communion of saints, the forgiveness of sins, the resurrection of the body, and the life everlasting. Amen.

🖐 Prayer Requests of the Week

Our Family

-
-
-
-

The Church

-
-
-
-

The World

-
-
-

🔊 The Lord's Prayer: Recite Together

Our Father which art in heaven, Hallowed be thy name. Thy kingdom come, Thy will be done in earth, as it is in heaven. Give us this day our daily bread. And forgive us our debts, as we forgive our debtors. And lead us not into temptation, but deliver us from evil: For thine is the kingdom, and the power, and the glory, forever. Amen.

♫ **Optional Singing:** Select a "psalm, hymn, or spiritual song" (Ephesians 5:19), from the Psalter, the church hymnal, or a Youtube worship playlist.

➡ Exercises For Children

In the free space on this page: (1) write out one of the catechism questions, (2) practice writing out or spelling some of the key words from the Scripture reading, or (3) draw a picture of something important from today's family discussion.

Family Activity Suggestion: Play some lawn games: bocce ball, lawn darts, and corn hole are cheap and fun. See Appendix #1 for other quality time ideas.

SERMON NOTES ON THIS WEEK'S TEXT

DATE

PREACHER

INTRODUCTION

MAIN IDEAS

PERSONAL or FAMILY APPLICATIONS

👆 **Opening Prayer (from the Book of Common Prayer). All pray together, or head of household may lead.**

Almighty God, to whom all hearts are open, all desires known, and from whom no secrets are hid; cleanse the thoughts of our hearts by the inspiration of Thy Holy Spirit, that we may more perfectly love Thee, and more worthily magnify Thy holy name, through Jesus Christ our Lord, Amen.

📖 **Scripture Reading: Mark 7:24-37 (ESV)**

24 And from there he arose and went away to the region of Tyre and Sidon. And he entered a house and did not want anyone to know, yet he could not be hidden. 25 But immediately a woman whose little daughter had an unclean spirit heard of him and came and fell down at his feet. 26 Now the woman was a Gentile, a Syrophoenician by birth. And she begged him to cast the demon out of her daughter. 27 And he said to her, "Let the children be fed first, for it is not right to take the children's bread and throw it to the dogs." 28 But she answered him, "Yes, Lord; yet even the dogs under the table eat the children's crumbs."29 And he said to her, "For this statement you may go your way; the demon has left your daughter." 30 And she went home and found the child lying in bed and the demon gone.

31 Then he returned from the region of Tyre and went through Sidon to the Sea of Galilee, in the region of the Decapolis. 32 And they brought to him a man who was deaf and had a speech impediment, and they begged him to lay his hand on him. 33 And taking him aside from the crowd privately, he put his fingers into his ears, and after spitting touched his tongue. 34 And looking up to heaven, he sighed and said to him, "Ephphatha," that is, "Be

opened." **35** And his ears were opened, his tongue was released, and he spoke plainly. **36** And Jesus charged them to tell no one. But the more he charged them, the more zealously they proclaimed it. **37** And they were astonished beyond measure, saying, "He has done all things well. He even makes the deaf hear and the mute speak."

▬ Scripture Reflection on Today's Reading

Put a circle around difficult words and phrases.

Put a star next to verses that cause us to praise and give thanks.

Underline verses with commands or that lead us to repent.

Put a box around key concepts and other family discussion points.

Westminster Catechism Questions

Q. 43. *What is the preface to the ten commandments?*
A. The preface to the ten commandments is in these words, I am the Lord thy God, which have brought thee out of the land of Egypt, out of the house of bondage.

Q. 44. *What doth the preface to the ten commandments teach us?*
A. The preface to the ten commandments teacheth us that because God is the Lord, and our God, and redeemer, therefore we are bound to keep all his commandments.

◀» Nicene Creed: Recite as a Family

We believe in one God, the Father Almighty, Maker of heaven and earth, and of all things visible and invisible.

And in one Lord Jesus Christ, the only-begotten Son of God, begotten of the Father before all worlds; God of God, Light of Light, very God of very God; begotten, not made, being of one substance with the Father, by whom all things were made. Who, for us and for our salvation, came down from heaven, and was incarnate by the Holy Spirit of the virgin Mary, and was made man; and was crucified also for us under Pontius Pilate; He suffered and was buried; and the third day He rose again, according to the Scriptures; and ascended into heaven, and sits on the right hand of the Father; and He shall come again, with glory, to judge the living and the dead; whose kingdom shall have no end.
And we believe in the Holy Ghost, the Lord and Giver of Life, who proceeds from the Father and the Son; who with the Father and the Son together is worshipped and glorified; who spoke by the prophets. And we believe in one holy catholic and apostolic Church. We acknowledge one baptism for the remission of sins; and we look for the resurrection of the dead, and the life of the world to come. Amen.

✋ Prayer Requests of the Week

Our Family

-

-

-

The Church

-

-

The World

-

-

🔊 The Lord's Prayer: Recite Together

Our Father which art in heaven, Hallowed be thy name. Thy kingdom come, Thy will be done in earth, as it is in heaven. Give us this day our daily bread. And forgive us our debts, as we forgive our debtors. And lead us not into temptation, but deliver us from evil: For thine is the kingdom, and the power, and the glory, forever. Amen.

🎵 **Optional Singing:** Select a "psalm, hymn, or spiritual song" (Ephesians 5:19), from the Psalter, the church hymnal, or a Youtube worship playlist.

🔖 Exercises For Children

In the free space on this page: (1) write out one of the catechism questions, (2) practice writing out or spelling some of the key words from the Scripture reading, or (3) draw a picture of something important from today's family discussion.

Family Activity Suggestion: Find a place to volunteer together. Or perform a simple act of mercy for a neighbor (raking leaves etc.) See Appendix #1 for other quality time ideas.

SERMON NOTES ON THIS WEEK'S TEXT

DATE

PREACHER

INTRODUCTION

MAIN IDEAS

PERSONAL or FAMILY APPLICATIONS

✋ Opening Prayer (from the Book of Common Prayer). All pray together, or head of household may lead.

Almighty God, to whom all hearts are open, all desires known, and from whom no secrets are hid; cleanse the thoughts of our hearts by the inspiration of Thy Holy Spirit, that we may more perfectly love Thee, and more worthily magnify Thy holy name, through Jesus Christ our Lord, Amen.

📖 Scripture Reading: Mark 8:1-13 (ESV)

In those days, when again a great crowd had gathered, and they had nothing to eat, he called his disciples to him and said to them, [2] "I have compassion on the crowd, because they have been with me now three days and have nothing to eat. [3] And if I send them away hungry to their homes, they will faint on the way. And some of them have come from far away." [4] And his disciples answered him, "How can one feed these people with bread here in this desolate place?" [5] And he asked them, "How many loaves do you have?" They said, "Seven."[6] And he directed the crowd to sit down on the ground. And he took the seven loaves, and having given thanks, he broke them and gave them to his disciples to set before the people; and they set them before the crowd. [7] And they had a few small fish. And having blessed them, he said that these also should be set before them. [8] And they ate and were satisfied. And they took up the broken pieces left over, seven baskets full. [9] And there were about four thousand people. And he sent them away. [10] And immediately he got into the boat with his disciples and went to the district of Dalmanutha.

[11] The Pharisees came and began to argue with him, seeking from him a sign from heaven to test him. [12] And he sighed deeply in his

spirit and said, "Why does this generation seek a sign? Truly, I say to you, no sign will be given to this generation." [13] And he left them, got into the boat again, and went to the other side.

⬤ Scripture Reflection on Today's Reading

Put a circle around difficult words and phrases.

Put a star next to verses that cause us to praise and give thanks.

Underline verses with commands or that lead us to repent.

Put a box around key concepts and other family discussion points.

◥ Westminster Catechism Questions

Q. 45. *Which is the first commandment?*
A. The first commandment is, Thou shalt have no other gods before me.

Q. 46. *What is required in the first commandment?*
A. The first commandment requireth us to know and acknowledge God to be the only true God, and our God; and to worship and glorify him accordingly.

◀» Ten Commandments: Recite as a Family

And God spake all these words, saying,
I am the Lord thy God, which have brought thee out of the land of Egypt, out of the house of bondage.
1. Thou shalt have no other gods before me.
2. Thou shalt not make unto thee any graven image, or any likeness of any thing that is in heaven above, or that is in the earth beneath, or that is in the water under the earth. Thou

shalt not bow down thyself to them, nor serve them: for I the Lord thy God am a jealous God, visiting the iniquity of the fathers upon the children unto the third and fourth generation of them that hate me; And shewing mercy unto thousands of them that love me, and keep my commandments.

3. Thou shalt not take the name of the Lord thy God in vain; for the Lord will not hold him guiltless that taketh his name in vain.

4. Remember the sabbath day, to keep it holy. Six days shalt thou labour, and do all thy work: But the seventh day is the sabbath of the Lord thy God: in it thou shalt not do any work, thou, nor thy son, nor thy daughter, thy manservant, nor thy maidservant, nor thy cattle, nor thy stranger that is within thy gates: For in six days the Lord made heaven and earth, the sea, and all that in them is, and rested the seventh day: wherefore the Lord blessed the sabbath day, and hallowed it.

5. Honour thy father and thy mother: that thy days may be long upon the land which the Lord thy God giveth thee.

6. Thou shalt not kill.

7. Thou shalt not commit adultery.

8. Thou shalt not steal.

9. Thou shalt not bear false witness against thy neighbour.

10. Thou shalt not covet thy neighbour's house, thou shalt not covet thy neighbour's wife, nor his manservant, nor his maidservant, nor his ox, nor his ass, nor any thing that is thy neighbour's.

🖐 Prayer Requests of the Week

Our Family

-

-

-

The Church

-

-

-

The World

-

-

-

🔊 **The Lord's Prayer: Recite Together**

Our Father which art in heaven, Hallowed be thy name. Thy kingdom come, Thy will be done in earth, as it is in heaven. Give us this day our daily bread. And forgive us our debts, as we forgive our debtors. And lead us not into temptation, but deliver us from evil: For thine is the kingdom, and the power, and the glory, forever. Amen.

🎵 **Optional Singing:** Select a "psalm, hymn, or spiritual song" (Ephesians 5:19), from the Psalter, the church hymnal, or a Youtube worship playlist.

➥ Exercises For Children

In the free space on this page: (1) write out one of the catechism questions, (2) practice writing out or spelling some of the key words from the Scripture reading, or (3) draw a picture of something important from today's family discussion.

Family Activity Suggestion: Fly a kite together. They are available at dollar stores, and fly well on a windy day! See Appendix #1 for other quality time ideas.

SERMON NOTES ON THIS WEEK'S TEXT

DATE

PREACHER

INTRODUCTION

MAIN IDEAS

PERSONAL or FAMILY APPLICATIONS

🕯 Call to Worship, Psalm 95 KJV
(Traditionally called the Venite Exultemus Domino)

[1] O come, let us sing unto the Lord: let us make a joyful noise to the rock of our salvation. [2] Let us come before his presence with thanksgiving, and make a joyful noise unto him with psalms. [3] For the Lord is a great God, and a great King above all gods. [4] In his hand are the deep places of the earth: the strength of the hills is his also. [5] The sea is his, and he made it: and his hands formed the dry land. [6] O come, let us worship and bow down: let us kneel before the Lord our maker. [7] For he is our God; and we are the people of his pasture, and the sheep of his hand.

📖 Scripture Reading: Mark 8:14-26 (NKJV)

[14] Now the disciples had forgotten to take bread, and they did not have more than one loaf with them in the boat. [15] Then He charged them, saying, "Take heed, beware of the leaven of the Pharisees and the leaven of Herod."
[16] And they reasoned among themselves, saying, "*It is* because we have no bread."
[17] But Jesus, being aware of *it,* said to them, "Why do you reason because you have no bread? Do you not yet perceive nor understand? Is your heart still hardened? [18] Having eyes, do you not see? And having ears, do you not hear? And do you not remember? [19] When I broke the five loaves for the five thousand, how many baskets full of fragments did you take up?"
They said to Him, "Twelve."
[20] "Also, when I broke the seven for the four thousand, how many large baskets full of fragments did you take up?"
And they said, "Seven."
[21] So He said to them, "How *is it* you do not understand?"

²² Then He came to Bethsaida; and they brought a blind man to Him, and begged Him to touch him. ²³ So He took the blind man by the hand and led him out of the town. And when He had spit on his eyes and put His hands on him, He asked him if he saw anything. ²⁴ And he looked up and said, "I see men like trees, walking." ²⁵ Then He put *His* hands on his eyes again and made him look up. And he was restored and saw everyone clearly. ²⁶ Then He sent him away to his house, saying, "Neither go into the town, nor tell anyone in the town."

➡ Scripture Reflection on Today's Reading

Put a circle around difficult words and phrases.

Put a star next to verses that cause us to praise and give thanks.

Underline verses with commands or that lead us to repent.

Put a box around key concepts and other family discussion points.

🎓 Westminster Catechism Questions

Q. 47. *What is forbidden in the first commandment?*
A. The first commandment forbiddeth the denying, or not worshiping and glorifying the true God as God, and our God; and the giving of that worship and glory to any other, which is due to him alone.

Q. 48. *What are we specially taught by these words before me in the first commandment?*
A. These words before me in the first commandment teach us that God, who seeth all things, taketh notice of, and is much displeased with, the sin of having any other god.

🔊 Heidelberg Catechism Question #1

Question 1. What is thy only comfort in life and death?

Answer: That I with body and soul, both in life and death, am not my own, but belong unto my faithful Saviour Jesus Christ; who, with his precious blood, has fully satisfied for all my sins, and delivered me from all the power of the devil; and so preserves me that without the will of my heavenly Father, not a hair can fall from my head; yea, that all things must be subservient to my salvation, and therefore, by his Holy Spirit, He also assures me of eternal life, and makes me sincerely willing and ready, henceforth, to live unto him.

🎵 **Optional Singing:** Select a "psalm, hymn, or spiritual song" (Ephesians 5:19), from the Psalter, the church hymnal, or a Youtube worship playlist.

✋ Prayer Requests of the Week

Our Family

-
-
-

The Church

-
-

-

The World

-

-

-

🔊 The Lord's Prayer: Recite Together

Our Father which art in heaven, Hallowed be thy name. Thy kingdom come, Thy will be done in earth, as it is in heaven. Give us this day our daily bread. And forgive us our debts, as we forgive our debtors. And lead us not into temptation, but deliver us from evil: For thine is the kingdom, and the power, and the glory, forever. Amen.

➡ Exercises For Children

In the free space on this page: (1) write out one of the catechism questions, (2) practice writing out or spelling some of the key words from the Scripture reading, or (3) draw a picture of something important from today's family discussion.

Family Activity Suggestion: Make a traditional picnic lunch, complete with blanket and wicker basket! See Appendix #1 for other quality time ideas.

SERMON NOTES ON THIS WEEK'S TEXT

DATE

PREACHER

INTRODUCTION

MAIN IDEAS

PERSONAL or FAMILY APPLICATIONS

🖐 **Opening Prayer (from the Book of Common Prayer). All pray together, or head of household may lead.**

Almighty God, to whom all hearts are open, all desires known, and from whom no secrets are hid; cleanse the thoughts of our hearts by the inspiration of Thy Holy Spirit, that we may more perfectly love Thee, and more worthily magnify Thy holy name, through Jesus Christ our Lord, Amen.

📖 **Scripture Reading: Mark 8:27 – 9:1 (ESV)**

27 And Jesus went on with his disciples to the villages of Caesarea Philippi. And on the way he asked his disciples, "Who do people say that I am?" 28 And they told him, "John the Baptist; and others say, Elijah; and others, one of the prophets." 29 And he asked them, "But who do you say that I am?" Peter answered him, "You are the Christ." 30 And he strictly charged them to tell no one about him.

31 And he began to teach them that the Son of Man must suffer many things and be rejected by the elders and the chief priests and the scribes and be killed, and after three days rise again. 32 And he said this plainly. And Peter took him aside and began to rebuke him. 33 But turning and seeing his disciples, he rebuked Peter and said, "Get behind me, Satan! For you are not setting your mind on the things of God, but on the things of man."
34 And calling the crowd to him with his disciples, he said to them, "If anyone would come after me, let him deny himself and take up his cross and follow me. 35 For whoever would save his life will lose it, but whoever loses his life for my sake and the gospel's will save it. 36 For what does it profit a man to gain the whole world and forfeit his soul? 37 For what can a man give in return for his

soul? [38] For whoever is ashamed of me and of my words in this adulterous and sinful generation, of him will the Son of Man also be ashamed when he comes in the glory of his Father with the holy angels."

[9:1] And he said to them, "Truly, I say to you, there are some standing here who will not taste death until they see the kingdom of God after it has come with power."

➡ Scripture Reflection on Today's Reading

Put a circle around difficult words and phrases.

Put a star next to verses that cause us to praise and give thanks.

Underline verses with commands or that lead us to repent.

Put a box around key concepts and other family discussion points.

🎓 Westminster Catechism Questions

Q. 49. *Which is the second commandment?*
A. The second commandment is, Thou shalt not make unto thee any graven image, or any likeness of anything that is in heaven above, or that is in the earth beneath, or that is in the water under the earth: thou shalt not bow down thyself to them, nor serve them: for I the Lord thy God am a jealous God, visiting the iniquity of the fathers upon the children unto the third and fourth generation of them that hate me; and showing mercy unto thousands of them that love me, and keep my commandments.

Q. 50. *What is required in the second commandment?*
A. The second commandment requireth the receiving, observing, and keeping pure and entire, all such religious worship and ordinances as God hath appointed in his word.

◀)) Apostle's Creed: Recite as a Family

I believe in God the Father Almighty, Maker of heaven and earth. I believe in Jesus Christ, His only Son, our Lord, who was conceived by the Holy Spirit, and born of the Virgin Mary. He suffered under Pontius Pilate, was crucified, died, and was buried; he descended into hell. The third day he rose again from the dead. He ascended into heaven, he is seated at the right hand of God the Father Almighty. From there he will come to judge the living and the dead. I believe in the Holy Spirit, the holy catholic church, the communion of saints, the forgiveness of sins, the resurrection of the body, and the life everlasting. Amen.

✋ Prayer Requests of the Week

Our Family

•

•

•

•

The Church

•

•

•

The World

-

-

🔊 The Lord's Prayer: Recite Together

Our Father which art in heaven, Hallowed be thy name. Thy kingdom come, Thy will be done in earth, as it is in heaven. Give us this day our daily bread. And forgive us our debts, as we forgive our debtors. And lead us not into temptation, but deliver us from evil: For thine is the kingdom, and the power, and the glory, forever. Amen.

🎵 **Optional Singing:** Select a "psalm, hymn, or spiritual song" (Ephesians 5:19), from the Psalter, the church hymnal, or a Youtube worship playlist.

✏ Exercises For Children

In the free space on this page: (1) write out one of the catechism questions, (2) practice writing out or spelling some of the key words from the Scripture reading, or (3) draw a picture of something important from today's family discussion.

Family Activity Suggestion: Make an evening bonfire with s'mores. Tell family stories and legends! See Appendix #1 for other quality time ideas.

SERMON NOTES ON THIS WEEK'S TEXT

DATE

PREACHER

INTRODUCTION

MAIN IDEAS

PERSONAL or FAMILY APPLICATIONS

🖐 **Opening Prayer (from the Book of Common Prayer). All pray together, or head of household may lead.**

Almighty God, to whom all hearts are open, all desires known, and from whom no secrets are hid; cleanse the thoughts of our hearts by the inspiration of Thy Holy Spirit, that we may more perfectly love Thee, and more worthily magnify Thy holy name, through Jesus Christ our Lord, Amen.

📖 **Scripture Reading: Mark 9:2-13 (ESV)**

[2] And after six days Jesus took with him Peter and James and John, and led them up a high mountain by themselves. And he was transfigured before them, [3] and his clothes became radiant, intensely white, as no one on earth could bleach them.[4] And there appeared to them Elijah with Moses, and they were talking with Jesus.[5] And Peter said to Jesus, "Rabbi, it is good that we are here. Let us make three tents, one for you and one for Moses and one for Elijah." [6] For he did not know what to say, for they were terrified. [7] And a cloud overshadowed them, and a voice came out of the cloud, "This is my beloved Son; listen to him." [8] And suddenly, looking around, they no longer saw anyone with them but Jesus only.

[9] And as they were coming down the mountain, he charged them to tell no one what they had seen, until the Son of Man had risen from the dead. [10] So they kept the matter to themselves, questioning what this rising from the dead might mean. [11] And they asked him, "Why do the scribes say that first Elijah must come?"[12] And he said to them, "Elijah does come first to restore all things. And how is it written of the Son of Man that he should suffer many things and be

treated with contempt? [13] But I tell you that Elijah has come, and they did to him whatever they pleased, as it is written of him."

➦ Scripture Reflection on Today's Reading

Put a circle around difficult words and phrases.

Put a star next to verses that cause us to praise and give thanks.

Underline verses with commands or that lead us to repent.

Put a box around key concepts and other family discussion points.

Westminster Catechism Questions

Q. 51. *What is forbidden in the second commandment?*
A. The second commandment forbiddeth the worshiping of God by images, or any other way not appointed in his word.

Q. 52. *What are the reasons annexed to the second commandment?*
A. The reasons annexed to the second commandment are, God's sovereignty over us, his propriety in us, and the zeal he hath to his own worship.

◀) Nicene Creed: Recite as a Family

We believe in one God, the Father Almighty, Maker of heaven and earth, and of all things visible and invisible.
And in one Lord Jesus Christ, the only-begotten Son of God, begotten of the Father before all worlds; God of God, Light of Light, very God of very God; begotten, not made, being of one substance with the Father, by whom all things were made. Who, for us and for our salvation, came down from heaven, and was incarnate by the

Holy Spirit of the virgin Mary, and was made man; and was crucified also for us under Pontius Pilate; He suffered and was buried; and the third day He rose again, according to the Scriptures; and ascended into heaven, and sits on the right hand of the Father; and He shall come again, with glory, to judge the living and the dead; whose kingdom shall have no end.
And we believe in the Holy Ghost, the Lord and Giver of Life, who proceeds from the Father and the Son; who with the Father and the Son together is worshipped and glorified; who spoke by the prophets. And we believe in one holy catholic and apostolic Church. We acknowledge one baptism for the remission of sins; and we look for the resurrection of the dead, and the life of the world to come. Amen.

✋ Prayer Requests of the Week

Our Family

-
-
-

The Church

-
-
-

The World

-
-
-

🔊 The Lord's Prayer: Recite Together

Our Father which art in heaven, Hallowed be thy name. Thy kingdom come, Thy will be done in earth, as it is in heaven. Give us this day our daily bread. And forgive us our debts, as we forgive our debtors. And lead us not into temptation, but deliver us from evil: For thine is the kingdom, and the power, and the glory, forever. Amen.

🎵 **Optional Singing:** Select a "psalm, hymn, or spiritual song" (Ephesians 5:19), from the Psalter, the church hymnal, or a Youtube worship playlist.

➡ Exercises For Children

In the free space on this page: (1) write out one of the catechism questions, (2) practice writing out or spelling some of the key words from the Scripture reading, or (3) draw a picture of something important from today's family discussion.

Family Activity Suggestion: Play "hide the penny" in the house. Penny must be at least partially visible! See Appendix #1 for other quality time ideas.

SERMON NOTES ON THIS WEEK'S TEXT

DATE

PREACHER

INTRODUCTION

MAIN IDEAS

PERSONAL or FAMILY APPLICATIONS

🔥 **Opening Prayer (from the Book of Common Prayer). All pray together, or head of household may lead.**

Almighty God, to whom all hearts are open, all desires known, and from whom no secrets are hid; cleanse the thoughts of our hearts by the inspiration of Thy Holy Spirit, that we may more perfectly love Thee, and more worthily magnify Thy holy name, through Jesus Christ our Lord, Amen.

📖 **Scripture Reading: Mark 9:14-32 (ESV)**

14 And when they came to the disciples, they saw a great crowd around them, and scribes arguing with them. 15 And immediately all the crowd, when they saw him, were greatly amazed and ran up to him and greeted him. 16 And he asked them, "What are you arguing about with them?" 17 And someone from the crowd answered him, "Teacher, I brought my son to you, for he has a spirit that makes him mute. 18 And whenever it seizes him, it throws him down, and he foams and grinds his teeth and becomes rigid. So I asked your disciples to cast it out, and they were not able." 19 And he answered them, "O faithless generation, how long am I to be with you? How long am I to bear with you? Bring him to me." 20 And they brought the boy to him. And when the spirit saw him, immediately it convulsed the boy, and he fell on the ground and rolled about, foaming at the mouth. 21 And Jesus asked his father, "How long has this been happening to him?" And he said, "From childhood. 22 And it has often cast him into fire and into water, to destroy him. But if you can do anything, have compassion on us and help us." 23 And Jesus said to him, "'If you can'! All things are possible for one who believes." 24 Immediately the father of the child cried out and said, "I believe; help my unbelief!" 25 And when Jesus saw that a crowd came running together, he rebuked the unclean spirit, saying to

it, "You mute and deaf spirit, I command you, come out of him and never enter him again." [26] And after crying out and convulsing him terribly, it came out, and the boy was like a corpse, so that most of them said, "He is dead." [27] But Jesus took him by the hand and lifted him up, and he arose. [28] And when he had entered the house, his disciples asked him privately, "Why could we not cast it out?" [29] And he said to them, "This kind cannot be driven out by anything but prayer."

[30] They went on from there and passed through Galilee. And he did not want anyone to know, [31] for he was teaching his disciples, saying to them, "The Son of Man is going to be delivered into the hands of men, and they will kill him. And when he is killed, after three days he will rise." [32] But they did not understand the saying, and were afraid to ask him.

➦ Scripture Reflection on Today's Reading

Put a circle around difficult words and phrases.

Put a star next to verses that cause us to praise and give thanks.

Underline verses with commands or that lead us to repent.

Put a box around key concepts and other family discussion points.

🎓 Westminster Catechism Questions

Q. 53. *Which is the third commandment?*
A. The third commandment is, Thou shalt not take the name of the Lord thy God in vain: for the Lord will not hold him guiltless that taketh his name in vain.

Q. 54. *What is required in the third commandment?*
A. The third commandment requireth the holy and reverent use of God's names, titles, attributes, ordinances, word and works.

🔊 Ten Commandments: Recite as a Family

And God spake all these words, saying,
I am the Lord thy God, which have brought thee out of the land of Egypt, out of the house of bondage.

1. Thou shalt have no other gods before me.
2. Thou shalt not make unto thee any graven image, or any likeness of any thing that is in heaven above, or that is in the earth beneath, or that is in the water under the earth. Thou shalt not bow down thyself to them, nor serve them: for I the Lord thy God am a jealous God, visiting the iniquity of the fathers upon the children unto the third and fourth generation of them that hate me; And shewing mercy unto thousands of them that love me, and keep my commandments.
3. Thou shalt not take the name of the Lord thy God in vain; for the Lord will not hold him guiltless that taketh his name in vain.
4. Remember the sabbath day, to keep it holy. Six days shalt thou labour, and do all thy work: But the seventh day is the sabbath of the Lord thy God: in it thou shalt not do any work, thou, nor thy son, nor thy daughter, thy manservant, nor thy maidservant, nor thy cattle, nor thy stranger that is within thy gates: For in six days the Lord made heaven and earth, the sea, and all that in them is, and rested the seventh day: wherefore the Lord blessed the sabbath day, and hallowed it.
5. Honour thy father and thy mother: that thy days may be long upon the land which the Lord thy God giveth thee.
6. Thou shalt not kill.
7. Thou shalt not commit adultery.

8. Thou shalt not steal.
9. Thou shalt not bear false witness against thy neighbour.
10. Thou shalt not covet thy neighbour's house, thou shalt not covet thy neighbour's wife, nor his manservant, nor his maidservant, nor his ox, nor his ass, nor any thing that is thy neighbour's.

✋ Prayer Requests of the Week

Our Family

-

-

-

The Church

-

-

-

The World

-

-

-

🔊 The Lord's Prayer: Recite Together

Our Father which art in heaven, Hallowed be thy name. Thy kingdom come, Thy will be done in earth, as it is in heaven. Give us this day our daily bread. And forgive us our debts, as we forgive our debtors. And lead us not into temptation, but deliver us from evil: For thine is the kingdom, and the power, and the glory, forever. Amen.

🎵 Optional Singing: Select a "psalm, hymn, or spiritual song" (Ephesians 5:19), from the Psalter, the church hymnal, or a Youtube worship playlist.

🔖 Exercises For Children

In the free space on this page: (1) write out one of the catechism questions, (2) practice writing out or spelling some of the key words from the Scripture reading, or (3) draw a picture of something important from today's family discussion.

Family Activity Suggestion: Play Frisbee or catch with mitts in the front yard. See Appendix #1 for other quality time ideas.

SERMON NOTES ON THIS WEEK'S TEXT

DATE

PREACHER

INTRODUCTION

MAIN IDEAS

PERSONAL or FAMILY APPLICATIONS

🖑 Call to Worship, Psalm 95 KJV
(Traditionally called the Venite Exultemus Domino)

[1] O come, let us sing unto the Lord: let us make a joyful noise to the rock of our salvation. [2] Let us come before his presence with thanksgiving, and make a joyful noise unto him with psalms. [3] For the Lord is a great God, and a great King above all gods. [4] In his hand are the deep places of the earth: the strength of the hills is his also. [5] The sea is his, and he made it: and his hands formed the dry land. [6] O come, let us worship and bow down: let us kneel before the Lord our maker. [7] For he is our God; and we are the people of his pasture, and the sheep of his hand.

📖 Scripture Reading: Mark 9:33-41 (ESV)

[33] And they came to Capernaum. And when he was in the house he asked them, "What were you discussing on the way?" [34] But they kept silent, for on the way they had argued with one another about who was the greatest. [35] And he sat down and called the twelve. And he said to them, "If anyone would be first, he must be last of all and servant of all." [36] And he took a child and put him in the midst of them, and taking him in his arms, he said to them, [37] "Whoever receives one such child in my name receives me, and whoever receives me, receives not me but him who sent me."

[38] John said to him, "Teacher, we saw someone casting out demons in your name, and we tried to stop him, because he was not following us." [39] But Jesus said, "Do not stop him, for no one who does a mighty work in my name will be able soon afterward to speak evil of me. [40] For the one who is not against us is for us. [41] For truly, I say to you, whoever gives you a cup of water to

drink because you belong to Christ will by no means lose his reward.

➡ Scripture Reflection on Today's Reading

Put a circle around difficult words and phrases.

Put a star next to verses that cause us to praise and give thanks.

Underline verses with commands or that lead us to repent.

Put a box around key concepts and other family discussion points.

🎓 Westminster Catechism Questions

Q. 55. *What is forbidden in the third commandment?*
A. The third commandment forbiddeth all profaning or abusing of anything whereby God maketh himself known.

Q. 56. *What is the reason annexed to the third commandment?*
A. The reason annexed to the third commandment is that however the breakers of this commandment may escape punishment from men, yet the Lord our God will not suffer them to escape his righteous judgment.

🔊 Heidelberg Catechism Question #1

Question 1. What is thy only comfort in life and death?

Answer: That I with body and soul, both in life and death, am not my own, but belong unto my faithful Saviour Jesus Christ; who, with his precious blood, has fully satisfied for all my sins, and delivered me from all the power of the devil; and so preserves me that without the will of my heavenly Father, not a hair can fall from my head; yea, that all things must be subservient to my salvation, and therefore, by his Holy Spirit, He also assures me of eternal life, and makes me sincerely willing and ready, henceforth, to live unto him.

✋ Prayer Requests of the Week

Our Family

-
-
-

The Church

-
-
-

The World

-
-
-

🔊 The Lord's Prayer: Recite Together

Our Father which art in heaven, Hallowed be thy name. Thy kingdom come, Thy will be done in earth, as it is in heaven. Give us this day our daily bread. And forgive us our debts, as we forgive our debtors. And lead us not into temptation, but deliver us from evil: For thine is the kingdom, and the power, and the glory, forever. Amen.

🎵 **Optional Singing:** Select a "psalm, hymn, or spiritual song" (Ephesians 5:19), from the Psalter, the church hymnal, or a Youtube worship playlist.

━ Exercises For Children

In the free space on this page: (1) write out one of the catechism questions, (2) practice writing out or spelling some of the key words from the Scripture reading, or (3) draw a picture of something important from today's family discussion.

Family Activity Suggestion: Make a phone call on speaker phone to your oldest living relative, and ask for a story of the "good old days." See Appendix #1 for other quality time ideas.

SERMON NOTES ON THIS WEEK'S TEXT

DATE

PREACHER

INTRODUCTION

MAIN IDEAS

PERSONAL or FAMILY APPLICATIONS

👆 Opening Prayer (from the Book of Common Prayer). All pray together, or head of household may lead.

Almighty God, to whom all hearts are open, all desires known, and from whom no secrets are hid; cleanse the thoughts of our hearts by the inspiration of Thy Holy Spirit, that we may more perfectly love Thee, and more worthily magnify Thy holy name, through Jesus Christ our Lord, Amen.

📖 Scripture Reading: Mark 9:42-50 (ESV)

[42] "Whoever causes one of these little ones who believe in me to sin, it would be better for him if a great millstone were hung around his neck and he were thrown into the sea. [43] And if your hand causes you to sin, cut it off. It is better for you to enter life crippled than with two hands to go to hell, to the unquenchable fire. [45] And if your foot causes you to sin, cut it off. It is better for you to enter life lame than with two feet to be thrown into hell. [47] And if your eye causes you to sin, tear it out. It is better for you to enter the kingdom of God with one eye than with two eyes to be thrown into hell, [48] 'where their worm does not die and the fire is not quenched.' [49] For everyone will be salted with fire. [50] Salt is good, but if the salt has lost its saltiness, how will you make it salty again? Have salt in yourselves, and be at peace with one another."

👄 Scripture Reflection on Today's Reading

Put a circle around difficult words and phrases.

Put a star next to verses that cause us to praise and give thanks.

Underline verses with commands or that lead us to repent.

Put a box around key concepts and other family discussion points.

◥ Westminster Catechism Questions

Q. 57. *Which is the fourth commandment?*
A. The fourth commandment is, Remember the sabbath day, to keep it holy. Six days shalt thou labor, and do all thy work: but the seventh day is the sabbath of the Lord thy God: in it thou shalt not do any work, thou, nor thy son, nor thy daughter, thy manservant, nor thy maidservant, nor thy cattle, nor thy stranger that is within thy gates: for in six days the Lord made heaven and earth, the sea, and all that in them is, and rested the seventh day: wherefore the Lord blessed the sabbath day, and hallowed it.

Q. 58. *What is required in the fourth commandment?*
A. The fourth commandment requireth the keeping holy to God such set times as he hath appointed in his word; expressly one whole day in seven, to be a holy sabbath to himself.

◀» Apostle's Creed: Recite as a Family

I believe in God the Father Almighty, Maker of heaven and earth. I believe in Jesus Christ, His only Son, our Lord, who was conceived by the Holy Spirit, and born of the Virgin Mary. He suffered under Pontius Pilate, was crucified, died, and was buried; he descended into hell. The third day he rose again from the dead. He ascended into heaven, he is seated at the right hand of God the Father Almighty. From there he will come to judge the living and the dead. I believe in the Holy Spirit, the holy catholic church, the communion of saints, the forgiveness of sins, the resurrection of the body, and the life everlasting. Amen.

✋ Prayer Requests of the Week

Our Family

-
-
-
-

The Church

-
-
-
-

The World

-
-
-

🔊 The Lord's Prayer: Recite Together

Our Father which art in heaven, Hallowed be thy name. Thy kingdom come, Thy will be done in earth, as it is in heaven. Give us this day our daily bread. And forgive us our debts, as we forgive our debtors. And lead us not into temptation, but deliver us from evil: For thine is the kingdom, and the power, and the glory, forever. Amen.

♪♪ **Optional Singing:** Select a "psalm, hymn, or spiritual song" (Ephesians 5:19), from the Psalter, the church hymnal, or a Youtube worship playlist.

━ Exercises For Children
In the free space on this page: (1) write out one of the catechism questions, (2) practice writing out or spelling some of the key words from the Scripture reading, or (3) draw a picture of something important from today's family discussion.

Family Activity Suggestion: Sit on the porch and attempt some bird watching. See how many different creatures you can identify. See Appendix #1 for other quality time ideas.

SERMON NOTES ON THIS WEEK'S TEXT

DATE

PREACHER

INTRODUCTION

MAIN IDEAS

PERSONAL or FAMILY APPLICATIONS

🕯 **Opening Prayer (from the Book of Common Prayer). All pray together, or head of household may lead.**

Almighty God, to whom all hearts are open, all desires known, and from whom no secrets are hid; cleanse the thoughts of our hearts by the inspiration of Thy Holy Spirit, that we may more perfectly love Thee, and more worthily magnify Thy holy name, through Jesus Christ our Lord, Amen.

📖 **Scripture Reading: Mark 10:1-16 (ESV)**

And he left there and went to the region of Judea and beyond the Jordan, and crowds gathered to him again. And again, as was his custom, he taught them.
2 And Pharisees came up and in order to test him asked, "Is it lawful for a man to divorce his wife?" 3 He answered them, "What did Moses command you?" 4 They said, "Moses allowed a man to write a certificate of divorce and to send her away." 5 And Jesus said to them, "Because of your hardness of heart he wrote you this commandment. 6 But from the beginning of creation, 'God made them male and female.' 7 'Therefore a man shall leave his father and mother and hold fast to his wife, 8 and the two shall become one flesh.' So they are no longer two but one flesh. 9 What therefore God has joined together, let not man separate."
10 And in the house the disciples asked him again about this matter. 11 And he said to them, "Whoever divorces his wife and marries another commits adultery against her, 12 and if she divorces her husband and marries another, she commits adultery."

13 And they were bringing children to him that he might touch them, and the disciples rebuked them. 14 But when Jesus saw it, he was indignant and said to them, "Let the children come to me; do not

hinder them, for to such belongs the kingdom of God. [15] Truly, I say to you, whoever does not receive the kingdom of God like a child shall not enter it." [16] And he took them in his arms and blessed them, laying his hands on them.

➡ Scripture Reflection on Today's Reading

Put a circle around difficult words and phrases.

Put a star next to verses that cause us to praise and give thanks.

Underline verses with commands or that lead us to repent.

Put a box around key concepts and other family discussion points.

Westminster Catechism Questions

Q. 59. *Which day of the seven hath God appointed to be the weekly sabbath?*
A. From the beginning of the world to the resurrection of Christ, God appointed the seventh day of the week to be the weekly sabbath; and the first day of the week ever since, to continue to the end of the world, which is the Christian sabbath.

Q. 60. *How is the sabbath to be sanctified?*
A. The sabbath is to be sanctified by a holy resting all that day, even from such worldly employments and recreations as are lawful on other days; and spending the whole time in the public and private exercises of God's worship, except so much as is to be taken up in the works of necessity and mercy.

◀ᴗ Nicene Creed: Recite as a Family

We believe in one God, the Father Almighty, Maker of heaven and earth, and of all things visible and invisible.

And in one Lord Jesus Christ, the only-begotten Son of God, begotten of the Father before all worlds; God of God, Light of Light, very God of very God; begotten, not made, being of one substance with the Father, by whom all things were made. Who, for us and for our salvation, came down from heaven, and was incarnate by the Holy Spirit of the virgin Mary, and was made man; and was crucified also for us under Pontius Pilate; He suffered and was buried; and the third day He rose again, according to the Scriptures; and ascended into heaven, and sits on the right hand of the Father; and He shall come again, with glory, to judge the living and the dead; whose kingdom shall have no end.

And we believe in the Holy Ghost, the Lord and Giver of Life, who proceeds from the Father and the Son; who with the Father and the Son together is worshipped and glorified; who spoke by the prophets. And we believe in one holy catholic and apostolic Church. We acknowledge one baptism for the remission of sins; and we look for the resurrection of the dead, and the life of the world to come. Amen.

✋ Prayer Requests of the Week

Our Family

-

-

-

The Church

-

-

-

The World

-

-

-

◀)) The Lord's Prayer: Recite Together

Our Father which art in heaven, Hallowed be thy name. Thy kingdom come, Thy will be done in earth, as it is in heaven. Give us this day our daily bread. And forgive us our debts, as we forgive our debtors. And lead us not into temptation, but deliver us from evil: For thine is the kingdom, and the power, and the glory, forever. Amen.

🎶 **Optional Singing:** Select a "psalm, hymn, or spiritual song" (Ephesians 5:19), from the Psalter, the church hymnal, or a Youtube worship playlist.

▬ Exercises For Children

In the free space on this page: (1) write out one of the catechism questions, (2) practice writing out or spelling some of the key words from the Scripture reading, or (3) draw a picture of something important from today's family discussion.

Family Activity Suggestion: Check through the prayer list at church and see if anyone is in the hospital. If so, visit them. If not, pray for any requests on the list anyway. See Appendix #1 for other quality time ideas.

SERMON NOTES ON THIS WEEK'S TEXT

DATE

PREACHER

INTRODUCTION

MAIN IDEAS

PERSONAL or FAMILY APPLICATIONS

🖐 **Opening Prayer (from the Book of Common Prayer). All pray together, or head of household may lead.**

Almighty God, to whom all hearts are open, all desires known, and from whom no secrets are hid; cleanse the thoughts of our hearts by the inspiration of Thy Holy Spirit, that we may more perfectly love Thee, and more worthily magnify Thy holy name, through Jesus Christ our Lord, Amen.

📖 **Scripture Reading: Mark 10:17-34 (ESV)**

[17] And as he was setting out on his journey, a man ran up and knelt before him and asked him, "Good Teacher, what must I do to inherit eternal life?" [18] And Jesus said to him, "Why do you call me good? No one is good except God alone. [19] You know the commandments: 'Do not murder, Do not commit adultery, Do not steal, Do not bear false witness, Do not defraud, Honor your father and mother.'" [20] And he said to him, "Teacher, all these I have kept from my youth." [21] And Jesus, looking at him, loved him, and said to him, "You lack one thing: go, sell all that you have and give to the poor, and you will have treasure in heaven; and come, follow me." [22] Disheartened by the saying, he went away sorrowful, for he had great possessions.
[23] And Jesus looked around and said to his disciples, "How difficult it will be for those who have wealth to enter the kingdom of God!" [24] And the disciples were amazed at his words. But Jesus said to them again, "Children, how difficult it is to enter the kingdom of God! [25] It is easier for a camel to go through the eye of a needle than for a rich person to enter the kingdom of God." [26] And they were exceedingly astonished, and said to him, "Then who can be saved?" [27] Jesus looked at them and said, "With man it is impossible, but not with God. For all things are possible with

God." [28] Peter began to say to him, "See, we have left everything and followed you." [29] Jesus said, "Truly, I say to you, there is no one who has left house or brothers or sisters or mother or father or children or lands, for my sake and for the gospel, [30] who will not receive a hundredfold now in this time, houses and brothers and sisters and mothers and children and lands, with persecutions, and in the age to come eternal life. [31] But many who are first will be last, and the last first."

[32] And they were on the road, going up to Jerusalem, and Jesus was walking ahead of them. And they were amazed, and those who followed were afraid. And taking the twelve again, he began to tell them what was to happen to him,[33] saying, "See, we are going up to Jerusalem, and the Son of Man will be delivered over to the chief priests and the scribes, and they will condemn him to death and deliver him over to the Gentiles. [34] And they will mock him and spit on him, and flog him and kill him. And after three days he will rise."

➡ Scripture Reflection on Today's Reading

Put a circle around difficult words and phrases.

Put a star next to verses that cause us to praise and give thanks.

Underline verses with commands or that lead us to repent.

Put a box around key concepts and other family discussion points.

🎓 Westminster Catechism Questions

Q. 61. *What is forbidden in the fourth commandment?*
A. The fourth commandment forbiddeth the omission or careless performance of the duties required, and the profaning the day by

idleness, or doing that which is in itself sinful, or by unnecessary thoughts, words or works, about our worldly employments or recreations.

Q. 62. *What are the reasons annexed to the fourth commandment?*
A. The reasons annexed to the fourth commandment are, God's allowing us six days of the week for our own employments, his challenging a special propriety in the seventh, his own example, and his blessing the sabbath day.

◀ Ten Commandments: Recite as a Family

And God spake all these words, saying,
I am the Lord thy God, which have brought thee out of the land of Egypt, out of the house of bondage.
1. Thou shalt have no other gods before me.
2. Thou shalt not make unto thee any graven image, or any likeness of any thing that is in heaven above, or that is in the earth beneath, or that is in the water under the earth. Thou shalt not bow down thyself to them, nor serve them: for I the Lord thy God am a jealous God, visiting the iniquity of the fathers upon the children unto the third and fourth generation of them that hate me; And shewing mercy unto thousands of them that love me, and keep my commandments.
3. Thou shalt not take the name of the Lord thy God in vain; for the Lord will not hold him guiltless that taketh his name in vain.
4. Remember the sabbath day, to keep it holy. Six days shalt thou labour, and do all thy work: But the seventh day is the sabbath of the Lord thy God: in it thou shalt not do any work, thou, nor thy son, nor thy daughter, thy manservant, nor thy maidservant, nor thy cattle, nor thy stranger that is within thy gates: For in six days the Lord made heaven and earth, the sea, and all that in them is, and rested the seventh day:

wherefore the Lord blessed the sabbath day, and hallowed it.

5. Honour thy father and thy mother: that thy days may be long upon the land which the Lord thy God giveth thee.
6. Thou shalt not kill.
7. Thou shalt not commit adultery.
8. Thou shalt not steal.
9. Thou shalt not bear false witness against thy neighbour.
10. Thou shalt not covet thy neighbour's house, thou shalt not covet thy neighbour's wife, nor his manservant, nor his maidservant, nor his ox, nor his ass, nor any thing that is thy neighbour's.

✋ Prayer Requests of the Week

Our Family

-
-
-

The Church

-
-
-

The World

-

•

•

🔊 The Lord's Prayer: Recite Together

Our Father which art in heaven, Hallowed be thy name. Thy kingdom come, Thy will be done in earth, as it is in heaven. Give us this day our daily bread. And forgive us our debts, as we forgive our debtors. And lead us not into temptation, but deliver us from evil: For thine is the kingdom, and the power, and the glory, forever. Amen.

🎵 **Optional Singing:** Select a "psalm, hymn, or spiritual song" (Ephesians 5:19), from the Psalter, the church hymnal, or a Youtube worship playlist.

➥ Exercises For Children
In the free space on this page: (1) write out one of the catechism questions, (2) practice writing out or spelling some of the key words from the Scripture reading, or (3) draw a picture of something important from today's family discussion.

Family Activity Suggestion: If you have not yet tried singing a Psalm from the psalter, try it today! Use a well-known tune such as Amazing Grace. See Appendix #1 for other quality time ideas.

SERMON NOTES ON THIS WEEK'S TEXT

DATE

PREACHER

INTRODUCTION

MAIN IDEAS

PERSONAL or FAMILY APPLICATIONS

174

✋ Call to Worship, Psalm 95 KJV
(Traditionally called the Venite Exultemus Domino)

¹ O come, let us sing unto the Lord: let us make a joyful noise to the rock of our salvation. ² Let us come before his presence with thanksgiving, and make a joyful noise unto him with psalms. ³ For the Lord is a great God, and a great King above all gods. ⁴ In his hand are the deep places of the earth: the strength of the hills is his also. ⁵ The sea is his, and he made it: and his hands formed the dry land. ⁶ O come, let us worship and bow down: let us kneel before the Lord our maker. ⁷ For he is our God; and we are the people of his pasture, and the sheep of his hand.

📖 Scripture Reading: Mark 10:35-45 (ESV)

³⁵ And James and John, the sons of Zebedee, came up to him and said to him, "Teacher, we want you to do for us whatever we ask of you." ³⁶ And he said to them, "What do you want me to do for you?" ³⁷ And they said to him, "Grant us to sit, one at your right hand and one at your left, in your glory." ³⁸ Jesus said to them, "You do not know what you are asking. Are you able to drink the cup that I drink, or to be baptized with the baptism with which I am baptized?" ³⁹ And they said to him, "We are able." And Jesus said to them, "The cup that I drink you will drink, and with the baptism with which I am baptized, you will be baptized, ⁴⁰ but to sit at my right hand or at my left is not mine to grant, but it is for those for whom it has been prepared." ⁴¹ And when the ten heard it, they began to be indignant at James and John. ⁴² And Jesus called them to him and said to them, "You know that those who are considered rulers of the Gentiles lord it over them, and their great ones exercise authority over them. ⁴³ But it shall not be so among you. But whoever would be great among you must be your servant, ⁴⁴ and whoever would be

first among you must be slave of all. ⁴⁵ For even the Son of Man came not to be served but to serve, and to give his life as a ransom for many."

☛ Scripture Reflection on Today's Reading

Put a circle around difficult words and phrases.

Put a star next to verses that cause us to praise and give thanks.

Underline verses with commands or that lead us to repent.

Put a box around key concepts and other family discussion points.

🎓 Westminster Catechism Questions

Q. 63. *Which is the fifth commandment?*
A. The fifth commandment is, Honor thy father and thy mother; that thy days may be long upon the land which the Lord thy God giveth thee.

Q. 64. *What is required in the fifth commandment?*
A. The fifth commandment requireth the preserving the honor, and performing the duties, belonging to every one in their several places and relations, as superiors, inferiors or equals.

🔊 Heidelberg Catechism Question #1

Question 1. What is thy only comfort in life and death?

Answer: That I with body and soul, both in life and death, am not my own, but belong unto my faithful Saviour Jesus Christ; who, with his precious blood, has fully satisfied for all my sins, and delivered me from all the power of the devil; and so preserves me that without the will of my heavenly Father, not a hair can fall from my head; yea, that all things must be subservient to my salvation, and therefore, by his Holy Spirit, He also assures me of eternal life, and makes me sincerely willing and ready, henceforth, to live unto him.

✋ Prayer Requests of the Week

Our Family

•

•

•

The Church

•

•

•

The World

•

•

•

🔊 The Lord's Prayer: Recite Together

Our Father which art in heaven, Hallowed be thy name. Thy kingdom come, Thy will be done in earth, as it is in heaven. Give us this day our daily bread. And forgive us our debts, as we forgive our debtors. And lead us not into temptation, but deliver us from evil: For thine is the kingdom, and the power, and the glory, forever. Amen.

🎵 **Optional Singing:** Select a "psalm, hymn, or spiritual song" (Ephesians 5:19), from the Psalter, the church hymnal, or a Youtube worship playlist.

🎺 **Exercises For Children**
In the free space on this page: (1) write out one of the catechism questions, (2) practice writing out or spelling some of the key words from the Scripture reading, or (3) draw a picture of something important from today's family discussion.

Family Activity Suggestion: Set out several "family heirlooms" and tell about how each one came into your family possession. See Appendix #1 for other quality time ideas.

SERMON NOTES ON THIS WEEK'S TEXT

DATE

PREACHER

INTRODUCTION

MAIN IDEAS

PERSONAL or FAMILY APPLICATIONS

☖ Opening Prayer (from the Book of Common Prayer). All pray together, or head of household may lead.

Almighty God, to whom all hearts are open, all desires known, and from whom no secrets are hid; cleanse the thoughts of our hearts by the inspiration of Thy Holy Spirit, that we may more perfectly love Thee, and more worthily magnify Thy holy name, through Jesus Christ our Lord, Amen.

▉ Scripture Reading: Mark 10:46-52 (ESV)

[46] And they came to Jericho. And as he was leaving Jericho with his disciples and a great crowd, Bartimaeus, a blind beggar, the son of Timaeus, was sitting by the roadside. [47] And when he heard that it was Jesus of Nazareth, he began to cry out and say, "Jesus, Son of David, have mercy on me!" [48] And many rebuked him, telling him to be silent. But he cried out all the more, "Son of David, have mercy on me!" [49] And Jesus stopped and said, "Call him." And they called the blind man, saying to him, "Take heart. Get up; he is calling you." [50] And throwing off his cloak, he sprang up and came to Jesus. [51] And Jesus said to him, "What do you want me to do for you?" And the blind man said to him, "Rabbi, let me recover my sight." [52] And Jesus said to him, "Go your way; your faith has made you well." And immediately he recovered his sight and followed him on the way.

☛ Scripture Reflection on Today's Reading

Put a circle around difficult words and phrases.

Put a star next to verses that cause us to praise and give thanks.

Underline verses with commands or that lead us to repent.

Put a box around key concepts and other family discussion points.

◥ Westminster Catechism Questions

Q. 65. *What is forbidden in the fifth commandment?*
A. The fifth commandment forbiddeth the neglecting of, or doing anything against, the honor and duty which belongeth to every one in their several places and relations.

Q. 66. *What is the reason annexed to the fifth commandment?*
A. The reason annexed to the fifth commandment is a promise of long life and prosperity (as far as it shall serve for God's glory and their own good) to all such as keep this commandment.

✋ Prayer Requests of the Week

Our Family

-

-

-

The Church

-

-

-

-

The World

-

-

-

🔊 The Lord's Prayer: Recite Together

Our Father which art in heaven, Hallowed be thy name. Thy kingdom come, Thy will be done in earth, as it is in heaven. Give us this day our daily bread. And forgive us our debts, as we forgive our debtors. And lead us not into temptation, but deliver us from evil: For thine is the kingdom, and the power, and the glory, forever. Amen.

🎶 **Optional Singing:** Select a "psalm, hymn, or spiritual song" (Ephesians 5:19), from the Psalter, the church hymnal, or a Youtube worship playlist.

✏️ Exercises For Children
In the free space on this page: (1) write out one of the catechism questions, (2) practice writing out or spelling some of the key words from the Scripture reading, or (3) draw a picture of something important from today's family discussion.

Family Activity Suggestion: Tell the story of how you personally came to faith in Christ for all to hear. See Appendix #1 for other quality time ideas.

SERMON NOTES ON THIS WEEK'S TEXT

DATE

PREACHER

INTRODUCTION

MAIN IDEAS

PERSONAL or FAMILY APPLICATIONS

Opening Prayer (from the Book of Common Prayer). All pray together, or head of household may lead.

Almighty God, to whom all hearts are open, all desires known, and from whom no secrets are hid; cleanse the thoughts of our hearts by the inspiration of Thy Holy Spirit, that we may more perfectly love Thee, and more worthily magnify Thy holy name, through Jesus Christ our Lord, Amen.

Scripture Reading: Mark 11:1-14 (ESV)

1 Now when they drew near to Jerusalem, to Bethphage and Bethany, at the Mount of Olives, Jesus sent two of his disciples ² and said to them, "Go into the village in front of you, and immediately as you enter it you will find a colt tied, on which no one has ever sat. Untie it and bring it. ³ If anyone says to you, 'Why are you doing this?' say, 'The Lord has need of it and will send it back here immediately.'" ⁴ And they went away and found a colt tied at a door outside in the street, and they untied it. ⁵ And some of those standing there said to them, "What are you doing, untying the colt?" ⁶ And they told them what Jesus had said, and they let them go. ⁷ And they brought the colt to Jesus and threw their cloaks on it, and he sat on it. ⁸ And many spread their cloaks on the road, and others spread leafy branches that they had cut from the fields. ⁹ And those who went before and those who followed were shouting, "Hosanna! Blessed is he who comes in the name of the Lord! ¹⁰ Blessed is the coming kingdom of our father David! Hosanna in the highest!"
¹¹ And he entered Jerusalem and went into the temple. And when he had looked around at everything, as it was already late, he went out to Bethany with the twelve.

[12] On the following day, when they came from Bethany, he was hungry. [13] And seeing in the distance a fig tree in leaf, he went to see if he could find anything on it. When he came to it, he found nothing but leaves, for it was not the season for figs. [14] And he said to it, "May no one ever eat fruit from you again." And his disciples heard it.

← Scripture Reflection on Today's Reading

Put a circle around difficult words and phrases.

Put a star next to verses that cause us to praise and give thanks.

Underline verses with commands or that lead us to repent.

Put a box around key concepts and other family discussion points.

🎓 Westminster Catechism Questions

Q. 67. *Which is the sixth commandment?*
A. The sixth commandment is, Thou shalt not kill.

Q. 68. *What is required in the sixth commandment?*
A. The sixth commandment requireth all lawful endeavors to preserve our own life, and the life of others.

🤚 Prayer Requests of the Week

Our Family

-

-

-
-

The Church

-
-
-
-

The World

-
-
-

🔊 **The Lord's Prayer: Recite Together**

Our Father which art in heaven, Hallowed be thy name. Thy kingdom come, Thy will be done in earth, as it is in heaven. Give us this day our daily bread. And forgive us our debts, as we forgive our debtors. And lead us not into temptation, but deliver us from evil: For thine is the kingdom, and the power, and the glory, forever. Amen.

♪ **Optional Singing:** Select a "psalm, hymn, or spiritual song" (Ephesians 5:19), from the Psalter, the church hymnal, or a Youtube worship playlist.

➖ Exercises For Children

In the free space on this page: (1) write out one of the catechism questions, (2) practice writing out or spelling some of the key words from the Scripture reading, or (3) draw a picture of something important from today's family discussion.

Family Activity Suggestion: Select a family activity that you have not yet done together from the Appendix at the end of this book.

SERMON NOTES ON THIS WEEK'S TEXT

DATE

PREACHER

INTRODUCTION

MAIN IDEAS

PERSONAL or FAMILY APPLICATIONS

🔥 **Opening Prayer (from the Book of Common Prayer). All pray together, or head of household may lead.**

Almighty God, to whom all hearts are open, all desires known, and from whom no secrets are hid; cleanse the thoughts of our hearts by the inspiration of Thy Holy Spirit, that we may more perfectly love Thee, and more worthily magnify Thy holy name, through Jesus Christ our Lord, Amen.

📖 **Scripture Reading: Mark 11:15-25 (NKJV)**

15 So they came to Jerusalem. Then Jesus went into the temple and began to drive out those who bought and sold in the temple, and overturned the tables of the money changers and the seats of those who sold doves. 16 And He would not allow anyone to carry wares through the temple. 17 Then He taught, saying to them, "Is it not written, 'My house shall be called a house of prayer for all nations'? But you have made it a 'den of thieves.' "
18 And the scribes and chief priests heard it and sought how they might destroy Him; for they feared Him, because all the people were astonished at His teaching. 19 When evening had come, He went out of the city.

20 Now in the morning, as they passed by, they saw the fig tree dried up from the roots. 21 And Peter, remembering, said to Him, "Rabbi, look! The fig tree which You cursed has withered away." 22 So Jesus answered and said to them, "Have faith in God. 23 For assuredly, I say to you, whoever says to this mountain, 'Be removed and be cast into the sea,' and does not doubt in his heart, but believes that those things he says will be done, he will have whatever he says. 24 Therefore I say to you, whatever things

you ask when you pray, believe that you receive *them,* and you will have *them.*

25 "And whenever you stand praying, if you have anything against anyone, forgive him, that your Father in heaven may also forgive you your trespasses.26 But if you do not forgive, neither will your Father in heaven forgive your trespasses."

➟ Scripture Reflection on Today's Reading

Put a circle around difficult words and phrases.

Put a star next to verses that cause us to praise and give thanks.

Underline verses with commands or that lead us to repent.

Put a box around key concepts and other family discussion points.

🎓 Westminster Catechism Questions

Q. 69. *What is forbidden in the sixth commandment?*
A. The sixth commandment forbiddeth the taking away of our own life, or the life of our neighbor unjustly, or whatsoever tendeth thereunto.

Q. 70. *Which is the seventh commandment?*
A. The seventh commandment is, Thou shalt not commit adultery.

✋ Prayer Requests of the Week

Our Family

-

-

-

-

The Church

-

-

-

-

The World

-

-

-

🔊 The Lord's Prayer: Recite Together

Our Father which art in heaven, Hallowed be thy name. Thy kingdom come, Thy will be done in earth, as it is in heaven. Give us this day our daily bread. And forgive us our debts, as we forgive our debtors. And lead us not into temptation, but deliver us from evil: For thine is the kingdom, and the power, and the glory, forever. Amen.

♪ **Optional Singing:** Select a "psalm, hymn, or spiritual song" (Ephesians 5:19), from the Psalter, the church hymnal, or a Youtube worship playlist.

▬ Exercises For Children

In the free space on this page: (1) write out one of the catechism questions, (2) practice writing out or spelling some of the key words from the Scripture reading, or (3) draw a picture of something important from today's family discussion.

Family Activity Suggestion: Select a family activity that you have not yet done together from the Appendix at the end of this book.

SERMON NOTES ON THIS WEEK'S TEXT

DATE

PREACHER

INTRODUCTION

MAIN IDEAS

PERSONAL or FAMILY APPLICATIONS

🖐 Call to Worship, Psalm 95 KJV
(Traditionally called the Venite Exultemus Domino)

¹ O come, let us sing unto the Lord: let us make a joyful noise to the rock of our salvation. ² Let us come before his presence with thanksgiving, and make a joyful noise unto him with psalms. ³ For the Lord is a great God, and a great King above all gods. ⁴ In his hand are the deep places of the earth: the strength of the hills is his also. ⁵ The sea is his, and he made it: and his hands formed the dry land. ⁶ O come, let us worship and bow down: let us kneel before the Lord our maker. ⁷ For he is our God; and we are the people of his pasture, and the sheep of his hand.

📖 Scripture Reading: Mark 11:27-33 (ESV)

²⁷ And they came again to Jerusalem. And as he was walking in the temple, the chief priests and the scribes and the elders came to him, ²⁸ and they said to him, "By what authority are you doing these things, or who gave you this authority to do them?" ²⁹ Jesus said to them, "I will ask you one question; answer me, and I will tell you by what authority I do these things. ³⁰ Was the baptism of John from heaven or from man? Answer me." ³¹ And they discussed it with one another, saying, "If we say, 'From heaven,' he will say, 'Why then did you not believe him?' ³² But shall we say, 'From man'?"— they were afraid of the people, for they all held that John really was a prophet. ³³ So they answered Jesus, "We do not know." And Jesus said to them, "Neither will I tell you by what authority I do these things."

➡ Scripture Reflection on Today's Reading

Put a circle around difficult words and phrases.

194

Put a star next to verses that cause us to praise and give thanks.

Underline verses with commands or that lead us to repent.

Put a box around key concepts and other family discussion points.

❦ Westminster Catechism Questions

Q. 71. *What is required in the seventh commandment?*
A. The seventh commandment requireth the preservation of our own and our neighbor's chastity, in heart, speech and behavior.

Q. 72. *What is forbidden in the seventh commandment?*
A. The seventh commandment forbiddeth all unchaste thoughts, words and actions.

✋ Prayer Requests of the Week

Our Family

-

-

-

-

The Church

-

-
-
-

The World

-
-
-

◀)) The Lord's Prayer: Recite Together

Our Father which art in heaven, Hallowed be thy name. Thy kingdom come, Thy will be done in earth, as it is in heaven. Give us this day our daily bread. And forgive us our debts, as we forgive our debtors. And lead us not into temptation, but deliver us from evil: For thine is the kingdom, and the power, and the glory, forever. Amen.

♫ Optional Singing: Select a "psalm, hymn, or spiritual song" (Ephesians 5:19), from the Psalter, the church hymnal, or a Youtube worship playlist.

➥ Exercises For Children

In the free space on this page: (1) write out one of the catechism questions, (2) practice writing out or spelling some of the key words from the Scripture reading, or (3) draw a picture of something important from today's family discussion.

Family Activity Suggestion: Select a family activity that you have not yet done together from the Appendix at the end of this book.

SERMON NOTES ON THIS WEEK'S TEXT

DATE

PREACHER

INTRODUCTION

MAIN IDEAS

PERSONAL or FAMILY APPLICATIONS

🖐 **Opening Prayer (from the Book of Common Prayer). All pray together, or head of household may lead.**

Almighty God, to whom all hearts are open, all desires known, and from whom no secrets are hid; cleanse the thoughts of our hearts by the inspiration of Thy Holy Spirit, that we may more perfectly love Thee, and more worthily magnify Thy holy name, through Jesus Christ our Lord, Amen.

📖 **Scripture Reading: Mark 12:1-17 (ESV)**

And he began to speak to them in parables. "A man planted a vineyard and put a fence around it and dug a pit for the winepress and built a tower, and leased it to tenants and went into another country. [2] When the season came, he sent a servant to the tenants to get from them some of the fruit of the vineyard.[3] And they took him and beat him and sent him away empty-handed. [4] Again he sent to them another servant, and they struck him on the head and treated him shamefully. [5] And he sent another, and him they killed. And so with many others: some they beat, and some they killed. [6] He had still one other, a beloved son. Finally he sent him to them, saying, 'They will respect my son.' [7] But those tenants said to one another, 'This is the heir. Come, let us kill him, and the inheritance will be ours.' [8] And they took him and killed him and threw him out of the vineyard. [9] What will the owner of the vineyard do? He will come and destroy the tenants and give the vineyard to others. [10] Have you not read this Scripture:
"'The stone that the builders rejected
　　has become the cornerstone;
[11] this was the Lord's doing,
　　and it is marvelous in our eyes'?"

[12] And they were seeking to arrest him but feared the people, for they perceived that he had told the parable against them. So they left him and went away.

[13] And they sent to him some of the Pharisees and some of the Herodians, to trap him in his talk. [14] And they came and said to him, "Teacher, we know that you are true and do not care about anyone's opinion. For you are not swayed by appearances, but truly teach the way of God. Is it lawful to pay taxes to Caesar, or not? Should we pay them, or should we not?" [15] But, knowing their hypocrisy, he said to them, "Why put me to the test? Bring me a denarius and let me look at it." [16] And they brought one. And he said to them, "Whose likeness and inscription is this?" They said to him, "Caesar's." [17] Jesus said to them, "Render to Caesar the things that are Caesar's, and to God the things that are God's." And they marveled at him.

➡ Scripture Reflection on Today's Reading

Put a circle around difficult words and phrases.

Put a star next to verses that cause us to praise and give thanks.

Underline verses with commands or that lead us to repent.

Put a box around key concepts and other family discussion points.

🎓 Westminster Catechism Questions

Q. 73. *Which is the eighth commandment?*
A. The eighth commandment is, Thou shalt not steal.

Q. 74. *What is required in the eighth commandment?*
A. The eighth commandment requireth the lawful procuring and furthering the wealth and outward estate of ourselves and others.

🖐 Prayer Requests of the Week

Our Family

-
-
-
-

The Church

-
-
-
-

The World

-
-
-

🔊 The Lord's Prayer: Recite Together

Our Father which art in heaven, Hallowed be thy name. Thy kingdom come, Thy will be done in earth, as it is in heaven. Give us this day our daily bread. And forgive us our debts, as we forgive our debtors. And lead us not into temptation, but deliver us from evil: For thine is the kingdom, and the power, and the glory, forever. Amen.

🎵 **Optional Singing:** Select a "psalm, hymn, or spiritual song" (Ephesians 5:19), from the Psalter, the church hymnal, or a Youtube worship playlist.

🔊 Exercises For Children
In the free space on this page: (1) write out one of the catechism questions, (2) practice writing out or spelling some of the key words from the Scripture reading, or (3) draw a picture of something important from today's family discussion.

Family Activity Suggestion: Select a family activity that you have not yet done together from the Appendix at the end of this book.

SERMON NOTES ON THIS WEEK'S TEXT

DATE

PREACHER

INTRODUCTION

MAIN IDEAS

PERSONAL or FAMILY APPLICATIONS

🔥 Call to Worship, Psalm 95 KJV
(Traditionally called the Venite Exultemus Domino)

[1] O come, let us sing unto the Lord: let us make a joyful noise to the rock of our salvation. [2] Let us come before his presence with thanksgiving, and make a joyful noise unto him with psalms. [3] For the Lord is a great God, and a great King above all gods. [4] In his hand are the deep places of the earth: the strength of the hills is his also. [5] The sea is his, and he made it: and his hands formed the dry land. [6] O come, let us worship and bow down: let us kneel before the Lord our maker. [7] For he is our God; and we are the people of his pasture, and the sheep of his hand.

📖 Scripture Reading: Mark 12:18-34 (ESV)

[18] And Sadducees came to him, who say that there is no resurrection. And they asked him a question, saying, [19] "Teacher, Moses wrote for us that if a man's brother dies and leaves a wife, but leaves no child, the man must take the widow and raise up offspring for his brother. [20] There were seven brothers; the first took a wife, and when he died left no offspring. [21] And the second took her, and died, leaving no offspring. And the third likewise. [22] And the seven left no offspring. Last of all the woman also died. [23] In the resurrection, when they rise again, whose wife will she be? For the seven had her as wife."
[24] Jesus said to them, "Is this not the reason you are wrong, because you know neither the Scriptures nor the power of God? [25] For when they rise from the dead, they neither marry nor are given in marriage, but are like angels in heaven. [26] And as for the dead being raised, have you not read in the book of Moses, in the passage about the bush, how God spoke to him, saying, 'I am the God of Abraham, and the God of Isaac, and the God of

Jacob'? [27] He is not God of the dead, but of the living. You are quite wrong."

[28] And one of the scribes came up and heard them disputing with one another, and seeing that he answered them well, asked him, "Which commandment is the most important of all?" [29] Jesus answered, "The most important is, 'Hear, O Israel: The Lord our God, the Lord is one. [30] And you shall love the Lord your God with all your heart and with all your soul and with all your mind and with all your strength.' [31] The second is this: 'You shall love your neighbor as yourself.' There is no other commandment greater than these." [32] And the scribe said to him, "You are right, Teacher. You have truly said that he is one, and there is no other besides him. [33] And to love him with all the heart and with all the understanding and with all the strength, and to love one's neighbor as oneself, is much more than all whole burnt offerings and sacrifices." [34] And when Jesus saw that he answered wisely, he said to him, "You are not far from the kingdom of God." And after that no one dared to ask him any more questions.

← Scripture Reflection on Today's Reading

Put a circle around difficult words and phrases.

Put a star next to verses that cause us to praise and give thanks.

Underline verses with commands or that lead us to repent.

Put a box around key concepts and other family discussion points.

◆ Westminster Catechism Questions

Q. 75. *What is forbidden in the eighth commandment?*
A. The eighth commandment forbiddeth whatsoever doth or may unjustly hinder our own or our neighbor's wealth or outward estate.

Q. 76. *Which is the ninth commandment?*
A. The ninth commandment is, Thou shalt not bear false witness against thy neighbor.

✋ Prayer Requests of the Week

Our Family

-
-
-
-

The Church

-
-
-
-

The World

-

-

-

🔊 The Lord's Prayer: Recite Together

Our Father which art in heaven, Hallowed be thy name. Thy kingdom come, Thy will be done in earth, as it is in heaven. Give us this day our daily bread. And forgive us our debts, as we forgive our debtors. And lead us not into temptation, but deliver us from evil: For thine is the kingdom, and the power, and the glory, forever. Amen.

🎵 **Optional Singing:** Select a "psalm, hymn, or spiritual song" (Ephesians 5:19), from the Psalter, the church hymnal, or a Youtube worship playlist.

➡ Exercises For Children
In the free space on this page: (1) write out one of the catechism questions, (2) practice writing out or spelling some of the key words from the Scripture reading, or (3) draw a picture of something important from today's family discussion.

Family Activity Suggestion: Select a family activity that you have not yet done together from the Appendix at the end of this book.

SERMON NOTES ON THIS WEEK'S TEXT

DATE

PREACHER

INTRODUCTION

MAIN IDEAS

PERSONAL or FAMILY APPLICATIONS

🖐 **Opening Prayer (from the Book of Common Prayer). All pray together, or head of household may lead.**

Almighty God, to whom all hearts are open, all desires known, and from whom no secrets are hid; cleanse the thoughts of our hearts by the inspiration of Thy Holy Spirit, that we may more perfectly love Thee, and more worthily magnify Thy holy name, through Jesus Christ our Lord, Amen.

📖 **Scripture Reading: Mark 12:35-44 (ESV)**

35 And as Jesus taught in the temple, he said, "How can the scribes say that the Christ is the son of David? 36 David himself, in the Holy Spirit, declared,

"'The Lord said to my Lord,
"Sit at my right hand,
    until I put your enemies under your feet."'
37 David himself calls him Lord. So how is he his son?" And the great throng heard him gladly.
Beware of the Scribes
38 And in his teaching he said, "Beware of the scribes, who like to walk around in long robes and like greetings in the marketplaces 39 and have the best seats in the synagogues and the places of honor at feasts, 40 who devour widows' houses and for a pretense make long prayers. They will receive the greater condemnation."

41 And he sat down opposite the treasury and watched the people putting money into the offering box. Many rich people put in large sums. 42 And a poor widow came and put in two small copper coins, which make a penny. 43 And he called his disciples to him and said to them, "Truly, I say to you, this poor widow has put in

more than all those who are contributing to the offering box. [44] For they all contributed out of their abundance, but she out of her poverty has put in everything she had, all she had to live on."

➾ Scripture Reflection on Today's Reading

Put a circle around difficult words and phrases.

Put a star next to verses that cause us to praise and give thanks.

Underline verses with commands or that lead us to repent.

Put a box around key concepts and other family discussion points.

🎓 Westminster Catechism Questions

Q. 77. *What is required in the ninth commandment?*
A. The ninth commandment requireth the maintaining and promoting of truth between man and man, and of our own and our neighbor's good name, especially in witness-bearing.

Q. 78. *What is forbidden in the ninth commandment?*
A. The ninth commandment forbiddeth whatsoever is prejudicial to truth, or injurious to our own or our neighbor's good name.

✋ Prayer Requests of the Week

Our Family

-
-

-

-

The Church

-

-

-

-

The World

-

-

-

🔊 The Lord's Prayer: Recite Together

Our Father which art in heaven, Hallowed be thy name. Thy kingdom come, Thy will be done in earth, as it is in heaven. Give us this day our daily bread. And forgive us our debts, as we forgive our debtors. And lead us not into temptation, but deliver us from evil: For thine is the kingdom, and the power, and the glory, forever. Amen.

🎵 **Optional Singing:** Select a "psalm, hymn, or spiritual song" (Ephesians 5:19), from the Psalter, the church hymnal, or a Youtube worship playlist.

➡ Exercises For Children

In the free space on this page: (1) write out one of the catechism questions, (2) practice writing out or spelling some of the key words from the Scripture reading, or (3) draw a picture of something important from today's family discussion.

Family Activity Suggestion: Select a family activity that you have not yet done together from the Appendix at the end of this book.

SERMON NOTES ON THIS WEEK'S TEXT

DATE

PREACHER

INTRODUCTION

MAIN IDEAS

PERSONAL or FAMILY APPLICATIONS

✋ Call to Worship, Psalm 95 KJV
(Traditionally called the Venite Exultemus Domino)

¹ O come, let us sing unto the Lord: let us make a joyful noise to the rock of our salvation. ² Let us come before his presence with thanksgiving, and make a joyful noise unto him with psalms. ³ For the Lord is a great God, and a great King above all gods. ⁴ In his hand are the deep places of the earth: the strength of the hills is his also. ⁵ The sea is his, and he made it: and his hands formed the dry land. ⁶ O come, let us worship and bow down: let us kneel before the Lord our maker. ⁷ For he is our God; and we are the people of his pasture, and the sheep of his hand.

📖 Scripture Reading: Mark 13:1-13 (ESV)

1 And as he came out of the temple, one of his disciples said to him, "Look, Teacher, what wonderful stones and what wonderful buildings!" ² And Jesus said to him, "Do you see these great buildings? There will not be left here one stone upon another that will not be thrown down."

³ And as he sat on the Mount of Olives opposite the temple, Peter and James and John and Andrew asked him privately, ⁴ "Tell us, when will these things be, and what will be the sign when all these things are about to be accomplished?" ⁵ And Jesus began to say to them, "See that no one leads you astray. ⁶ Many will come in my name, saying, 'I am he!' and they will lead many astray. ⁷ And when you hear of wars and rumors of wars, do not be alarmed. This must take place, but the end is not yet. ⁸ For nation will rise against nation, and kingdom against kingdom. There will

be earthquakes in various places; there will be famines. These are but the beginning of the birth pains.

[9] "But be on your guard. For they will deliver you over to councils, and you will be beaten in synagogues, and you will stand before governors and kings for my sake, to bear witness before them. [10] And the gospel must first be proclaimed to all nations. [11] And when they bring you to trial and deliver you over, do not be anxious beforehand what you are to say, but say whatever is given you in that hour, for it is not you who speak, but the Holy Spirit. [12] And brother will deliver brother over to death, and the father his child, and children will rise against parents and have them put to death. [13] And you will be hated by all for my name's sake. But the one who endures to the end will be saved.

➦ Scripture Reflection on Today's Reading

Put a circle around difficult words and phrases.

Put a star next to verses that cause us to praise and give thanks.

Underline verses with commands or that lead us to repent.

Put a box around key concepts and other family discussion points.

◣ Westminster Catechism Questions

Q. 79. *Which is the tenth commandment?*
A. The tenth commandment is, Thou shalt not covet thy neighbor's house, thou shalt not covet thy neighbor's wife, nor his manservant, nor his maidservant, nor his ox, nor his ass, nor anything that is thy neighbor's.

Q. 80. *What is required in the tenth commandment?*
A. The tenth commandment requireth full contentment with our own condition, with a right and charitable frame of spirit toward our neighbor, and all that is his.

✋ Prayer Requests of the Week

Our Family

-
-
-
-

The Church

-
-
-
-

The World

-
-

●

🔊 The Lord's Prayer: Recite Together

Our Father which art in heaven, Hallowed be thy name. Thy kingdom come, Thy will be done in earth, as it is in heaven. Give us this day our daily bread. And forgive us our debts, as we forgive our debtors. And lead us not into temptation, but deliver us from evil: For thine is the kingdom, and the power, and the glory, forever. Amen.

🎵 **Optional Singing:** Select a "psalm, hymn, or spiritual song" (Ephesians 5:19), from the Psalter, the church hymnal, or a Youtube worship playlist.

➡ Exercises For Children

In the free space on this page: (1) write out one of the catechism questions, (2) practice writing out or spelling some of the key words from the Scripture reading, or (3) draw a picture of something important from today's family discussion.

Family Activity Suggestion: Select a family activity that you have not yet done together from the Appendix at the end of this book.

SERMON NOTES ON THIS WEEK'S TEXT

DATE

PREACHER

INTRODUCTION

MAIN IDEAS

PERSONAL or FAMILY APPLICATIONS

🕯 **Opening Prayer (from the Book of Common Prayer). All pray together, or head of household may lead.**

Almighty God, to whom all hearts are open, all desires known, and from whom no secrets are hid; cleanse the thoughts of our hearts by the inspiration of Thy Holy Spirit, that we may more perfectly love Thee, and more worthily magnify Thy holy name, through Jesus Christ our Lord, Amen.

📖 **Scripture Reading: Mark 13:14-27 (ESV)**

14 "But when you see the abomination of desolation standing where he ought not to be (let the reader understand), then let those who are in Judea flee to the mountains. 15 Let the one who is on the housetop not go down, nor enter his house, to take anything out, 16 and let the one who is in the field not turn back to take his cloak. 17 And alas for women who are pregnant and for those who are nursing infants in those days! 18 Pray that it may not happen in winter. 19 For in those days there will be such tribulation as has not been from the beginning of the creation that God created until now, and never will be. 20 And if the Lord had not cut short the days, no human being would be saved. But for the sake of the elect, whom he chose, he shortened the days. 21 And then if anyone says to you, 'Look, here is the Christ!' or 'Look, there he is!' do not believe it. 22 For false christs and false prophets will arise and perform signs and wonders, to lead astray, if possible, the elect. 23 But be on guard; I have told you all things beforehand.

24 "But in those days, after that tribulation, the sun will be darkened, and the moon will not give its light, 25 and the stars will be falling from heaven, and the powers in the heavens will be shaken. 26 And then they will see the Son of Man coming in clouds with great

power and glory. [27] And then he will send out the angels and gather his elect from the four winds, from the ends of the earth to the ends of heaven.

➡ Scripture Reflection on Today's Reading

Put a circle around difficult words and phrases.

Put a star next to verses that cause us to praise and give thanks.

Underline verses with commands or that lead us to repent.

Put a box around key concepts and other family discussion points.

🎓 Westminster Catechism Questions

Q. 81. *What is forbidden in the tenth commandment?*
A. The tenth commandment forbiddeth all discontentment with our own estate, envying or grieving at the good of our neighbor, and all inordinate motions and affections to anything that is his.

Q. 82. *Is any man able perfectly to keep the commandments of God?*
A. No mere man since the fall is able in this life perfectly to keep the commandments of God, but doth daily break them in thought, word and deed.

✋ Prayer Requests of the Week

Our Family

-
-

-

-

The Church

-

-

-

-

The World

-

-

-

🔊 **The Lord's Prayer: Recite Together**

Our Father which art in heaven, Hallowed be thy name. Thy kingdom come, Thy will be done in earth, as it is in heaven. Give us this day our daily bread. And forgive us our debts, as we forgive our debtors. And lead us not into temptation, but deliver us from evil: For thine is the kingdom, and the power, and the glory, forever. Amen.

♪ **Optional Singing:** Select a "psalm, hymn, or spiritual song" (Ephesians 5:19), from the Psalter, the church hymnal, or a Youtube worship playlist.

━ Exercises For Children

In the free space on this page: (1) write out one of the catechism questions, (2) practice writing out or spelling some of the key words from the Scripture reading, or (3) draw a picture of something important from today's family discussion.

Family Activity Suggestion: Select a family activity that you have not yet done together from the Appendix at the end of this book.

SERMON NOTES ON THIS WEEK'S TEXT

DATE

PREACHER

INTRODUCTION

MAIN IDEAS

PERSONAL or FAMILY APPLICATIONS

✋ Opening Prayer (from the Book of Common Prayer). All pray together, or head of household may lead.

Almighty God, to whom all hearts are open, all desires known, and from whom no secrets are hid; cleanse the thoughts of our hearts by the inspiration of Thy Holy Spirit, that we may more perfectly love Thee, and more worthily magnify Thy holy name, through Jesus Christ our Lord, Amen.

📖 Scripture Reading: Mark 13:28-37 (ESV)

28 "From the fig tree learn its lesson: as soon as its branch becomes tender and puts out its leaves, you know that summer is near. 29 So also, when you see these things taking place, you know that he is near, at the very gates. 30 Truly, I say to you, this generation will not pass away until all these things take place. 31 Heaven and earth will pass away, but my words will not pass away.

32 "But concerning that day or that hour, no one knows, not even the angels in heaven, nor the Son, but only the Father. 33 Be on guard, keep awake. For you do not know when the time will come. 34 It is like a man going on a journey, when he leaves home and puts his servants in charge, each with his work, and commands the doorkeeper to stay awake. 35 Therefore stay awake—for you do not know when the master of the house will come, in the evening, or at midnight, or when the rooster crows, or in the morning— 36 lest he come suddenly and find you asleep. 37 And what I say to you I say to all: Stay awake."

➡ Scripture Reflection on Today's Reading

Put a circle around difficult words and phrases.

Put a star next to verses that cause us to praise and give thanks.

Underline verses with commands or that lead us to repent.

Put a box around key concepts and other family discussion points.

◗ Westminster Catechism Questions

Q. 83. *Are all transgressions of the law equally heinous?*
A. Some sins in themselves, and by reason of several aggravations, are more heinous in the sight of God than others.

Q. 84. *What doth every sin deserve?*
A. Every sin deserveth God's wrath and curse, both in this life, and that which is to come.

✋ Prayer Requests of the Week

Our Family

-
-
-
-

The Church

-

-

-

-

The World

-

-

-

🔊 **The Lord's Prayer: Recite Together**

Our Father which art in heaven, Hallowed be thy name. Thy kingdom come, Thy will be done in earth, as it is in heaven. Give us this day our daily bread. And forgive us our debts, as we forgive our debtors. And lead us not into temptation, but deliver us from evil: For thine is the kingdom, and the power, and the glory, forever. Amen.

🎶 **Optional Singing:** Select a "psalm, hymn, or spiritual song" (Ephesians 5:19), from the Psalter, the church hymnal, or a Youtube worship playlist.

➡ Exercises For Children

In the free space on this page: (1) write out one of the catechism questions, (2) practice writing out or spelling some of the key words from the Scripture reading, or (3) draw a picture of something important from today's family discussion.

Family Activity: Select a family activity that you have not yet done together from the Appendix at the end of this book.

SERMON NOTES ON THIS WEEK'S TEXT

DATE

PREACHER

INTRODUCTION

MAIN IDEAS

PERSONAL or FAMILY APPLICATIONS

🖐 **Opening Prayer (from the Book of Common Prayer). All pray together, or head of household may lead.**

Almighty God, to whom all hearts are open, all desires known, and from whom no secrets are hid; cleanse the thoughts of our hearts by the inspiration of Thy Holy Spirit, that we may more perfectly love Thee, and more worthily magnify Thy holy name, through Jesus Christ our Lord, Amen.

📖 **Scripture Reading: Mark 14:1-10 (ESV)**

1 It was now two days before the Passover and the Feast of Unleavened Bread. And the chief priests and the scribes were seeking how to arrest him by stealth and kill him, [2] for they said, "Not during the feast, lest there be an uproar from the people."

[3] And while he was at Bethany in the house of Simon the leper, as he was reclining at table, a woman came with an alabaster flask of ointment of pure nard, very costly, and she broke the flask and poured it over his head. [4] There were some who said to themselves indignantly, "Why was the ointment wasted like that? [5] For this ointment could have been sold for more than three hundred denarii and given to the poor." And they scolded her. [6] But Jesus said, "Leave her alone. Why do you trouble her? She has done a beautiful thing to me. [7] For you always have the poor with you, and whenever you want, you can do good for them. But you will not always have me. [8] She has done what she could; she has anointed my body beforehand for burial. [9] And truly, I say to you, wherever the gospel is proclaimed in the whole world, what she has done will be told in memory of her."
[10] Then Judas Iscariot, who was one of the twelve, went to the chief priests in order to betray him to them. [11] And when they heard it,

they were glad and promised to give him money. And he sought an opportunity to betray him.

➡ Scripture Reflection on Today's Reading

Put a circle around difficult words and phrases.

Put a star next to verses that cause us to praise and give thanks.

Underline verses with commands or that lead us to repent.

Put a box around key concepts and other family discussion points.

🎓 Westminster Catechism Questions

Q. 85. *What doth God require of us that we may escape his wrath and curse due to us for sin?*
A. To escape the wrath and curse of God due to us for sin, God requireth of us faith in Jesus Christ, repentance unto life, with the diligent use of all the outward means whereby Christ communicateth to us the benefits of redemption.

Q. 86. *What is faith in Jesus Christ?*
A. Faith in Jesus Christ is a saving grace, whereby we receive and rest upon him alone for salvation, as he is offered to us in the gospel.

✋ Prayer Requests of the Week

Our Family

*

*

-

-

The Church

-

-

-

-

The World

-

-

-

🔊 **The Lord's Prayer: Recite Together**

Our Father which art in heaven, Hallowed be thy name. Thy kingdom come, Thy will be done in earth, as it is in heaven. Give us this day our daily bread. And forgive us our debts, as we forgive our debtors. And lead us not into temptation, but deliver us from evil: For thine is the kingdom, and the power, and the glory, forever. Amen.

♪ **Optional Singing:** Select a "psalm, hymn, or spiritual song" (Ephesians 5:19), from the Psalter, the church hymnal, or a Youtube worship playlist.

➥ Exercises For Children

In the free space on this page: (1) write out one of the catechism questions, (2) practice writing out or spelling some of the key words from the Scripture reading, or (3) draw a picture of something important from today's family discussion.

Family Activity: See Appendix #1 for quality time ideas.

SERMON NOTES ON THIS WEEK'S TEXT

DATE

PREACHER

INTRODUCTION

MAIN IDEAS

PERSONAL or FAMILY APPLICATIONS

✋ Call to Worship, Psalm 95 KJV
(Traditionally called the Venite Exultemus Domino)

[1] O come, let us sing unto the Lord: let us make a joyful noise to the rock of our salvation. [2] Let us come before his presence with thanksgiving, and make a joyful noise unto him with psalms. [3] For the Lord is a great God, and a great King above all gods. [4] In his hand are the deep places of the earth: the strength of the hills is his also. [5] The sea is his, and he made it: and his hands formed the dry land. [6] O come, let us worship and bow down: let us kneel before the Lord our maker. [7] For he is our God; and we are the people of his pasture, and the sheep of his hand.

📖 Scripture Reading: Mark 14:12-25 (ESV)

And on the first day of Unleavened Bread, when they sacrificed the Passover lamb, his disciples said to him, "Where will you have us go and prepare for you to eat the Passover?" [13] And he sent two of his disciples and said to them, "Go into the city, and a man carrying a jar of water will meet you. Follow him, [14] and wherever he enters, say to the master of the house, 'The Teacher says, Where is my guest room, where I may eat the Passover with my disciples?' [15] And he will show you a large upper room furnished and ready; there prepare for us." [16] And the disciples set out and went to the city and found it just as he had told them, and they prepared the Passover.

[17] And when it was evening, he came with the twelve. [18] And as they were reclining at table and eating, Jesus said, "Truly, I say to you, one of you will betray me, one who is eating with me." [19] They began to be sorrowful and to say to him one after another, "Is it

I?" [20] He said to them, "It is one of the twelve, one who is dipping
bread into the dish with me. [21] For the Son of Man goes as it is
written of him, but woe to that man by whom the Son of Man is
betrayed! It would have been better for that man if he had not been
born."
[22] And as they were eating, he took bread, and after blessing it
broke it and gave it to them, and said, "Take; this is my
body." [23] And he took a cup, and when he had given thanks he
gave it to them, and they all drank of it. [24] And he said to
them, "This is my blood of the covenant, which is poured out
for many. [25] Truly, I say to you, I will not drink again of the fruit of
the vine until that day when I drink it new in the kingdom of God."

Scripture Reflection on Today's Reading

Put a circle around difficult words and phrases.

Put a star next to verses that cause us to praise and give thanks.

Underline verses with commands or that lead us to repent.

Put a box around key concepts and other family discussion points.

Westminster Catechism Questions

Q. 87. *What is repentance unto life?*
A. Repentance unto life is a saving grace, whereby a sinner, out of a true sense of his sin, and apprehension of the mercy of God in Christ, doth, with grief and hatred of his sin, turn from it unto God, with full purpose of, and endeavor after, new obedience.

Q. 88. *What are the outward and ordinary means whereby Christ communicateth to us the benefits of redemption?*
A. The outward and ordinary means whereby Christ communicateth

to us the benefits of redemption, are his ordinances, especially the word, sacraments, and prayer; all which are made effectual to the elect for salvation.

✋ Prayer Requests of the Week

Our Family

-

-

-

-

The Church

-

-

-

-

The World

-

-

-

🔊 The Lord's Prayer: Recite Together

Our Father which art in heaven, Hallowed be thy name. Thy kingdom come, Thy will be done in earth, as it is in heaven. Give us this day our daily bread. And forgive us our debts, as we forgive our debtors. And lead us not into temptation, but deliver us from evil: For thine is the kingdom, and the power, and the glory, forever. Amen.

♪♪ **Optional Singing:** Select a "psalm, hymn, or spiritual song" (Ephesians 5:19), from the Psalter, the church hymnal, or a Youtube worship playlist.

■ Exercises For Children

In the free space on this page: (1) write out one of the catechism questions, (2) practice writing out or spelling some of the key words from the Scripture reading, or (3) draw a picture of something important from today's family discussion.

Family Activity: See Appendix #1 for quality time ideas.

SERMON NOTES ON THIS WEEK'S TEXT

DATE

PREACHER

INTRODUCTION

MAIN IDEAS

PERSONAL or FAMILY APPLICATIONS

🖐 **Opening Prayer (from the Book of Common Prayer). All pray together, or head of household may lead.**

Almighty God, to whom all hearts are open, all desires known, and from whom no secrets are hid; cleanse the thoughts of our hearts by the inspiration of Thy Holy Spirit, that we may more perfectly love Thee, and more worthily magnify Thy holy name, through Jesus Christ our Lord, Amen.

📖 **Scripture Reading: Mark 14:26-42 (ESV)**

26 And when they had sung a hymn, they went out to the Mount of Olives. 27 And Jesus said to them, "You will all fall away, for it is written, 'I will strike the shepherd, and the sheep will be scattered.' 28 But after I am raised up, I will go before you to Galilee." 29 Peter said to him, "Even though they all fall away, I will not." 30 And Jesus said to him, "Truly, I tell you, this very night, before the rooster crows twice, you will deny me three times." 31 But he said emphatically, "If I must die with you, I will not deny you." And they all said the same.

32 And they went to a place called Gethsemane. And he said to his disciples, "Sit here while I pray." 33 And he took with him Peter and James and John, and began to be greatly distressed and troubled. 34 And he said to them, "My soul is very sorrowful, even to death. Remain here and watch." 35 And going a little farther, he fell on the ground and prayed that, if it were possible, the hour might pass from him. 36 And he said, "Abba, Father, all things are possible for you. Remove this cup from me. Yet not what I will, but what you will." 37 And he came and found them sleeping, and he said to Peter, "Simon, are you asleep? Could you not watch one hour? 38 Watch and pray that you may not enter into temptation.

The spirit indeed is willing, but the flesh is weak." **39** And again he went away and prayed, saying the same words. **40** And again he came and found them sleeping, for their eyes were very heavy, and they did not know what to answer him. **41** And he came the third time and said to them, "Are you still sleeping and taking your rest? It is enough; the hour has come. The Son of Man is betrayed into the hands of sinners. **42** Rise, let us be going; see, my betrayer is at hand."

➡ Scripture Reflection on Today's Reading

Put a circle around difficult words and phrases.

Put a star next to verses that cause us to praise and give thanks.

Underline verses with commands or that lead us to repent.

Put a box around key concepts and other family discussion points.

🎓 Westminster Catechism Questions

Q. 89. *How is the word made effectual to salvation?*
A. The Spirit of God maketh the reading, but especially the preaching, of the word, an effectual means of convincing and converting sinners, and of building them up in holiness and comfort, through faith, unto salvation.

Q. 90. *How is the word to be read and heard, that it may become effectual to salvation?*
A. That the word may become effectual to salvation, we must attend thereunto with diligence, preparation and prayer; receive it with faith and love, lay it up in our hearts, and practice it in our lives.

✋ Prayer Requests of the Week

Our Family

-
-
-
-

The Church

-
-
-
-

The World

-
-
-

🔊 The Lord's Prayer: Recite Together

Our Father which art in heaven, Hallowed be thy name. Thy kingdom come, Thy will be done in earth, as it is in heaven. Give us this day our daily bread. And forgive us our debts, as we forgive our debtors. And lead us not into temptation, but deliver us from evil: For thine is the kingdom, and the power, and the glory, forever. Amen.

🎵 **Optional Singing:** Select a "psalm, hymn, or spiritual song" (Ephesians 5:19), from the Psalter, the church hymnal, or a Youtube worship playlist.

━ **Exercises For Children**
In the free space on this page: (1) write out one of the catechism questions, (2) practice writing out or spelling some of the key words from the Scripture reading, or (3) draw a picture of something important from today's family discussion.

Family Activity: See Appendix #1 for quality time ideas.

SERMON NOTES ON THIS WEEK'S TEXT

DATE

PREACHER

INTRODUCTION

MAIN IDEAS

PERSONAL or FAMILY APPLICATIONS

🖐 **Opening Prayer (from the Book of Common Prayer). All pray together, or head of household may lead.**

Almighty God, to whom all hearts are open, all desires known, and from whom no secrets are hid; cleanse the thoughts of our hearts by the inspiration of Thy Holy Spirit, that we may more perfectly love Thee, and more worthily magnify Thy holy name, through Jesus Christ our Lord, Amen.

📖 **Scripture Reading: Mark 14:43-65 (ESV)**

43 And immediately, while he was still speaking, Judas came, one of the twelve, and with him a crowd with swords and clubs, from the chief priests and the scribes and the elders. 44 Now the betrayer had given them a sign, saying, "The one I will kiss is the man. Seize him and lead him away under guard." 45 And when he came, he went up to him at once and said, "Rabbi!" And he kissed him. 46 And they laid hands on him and seized him. 47 But one of those who stood by drew his sword and struck the servant of the high priest and cut off his ear. 48 And Jesus said to them, "Have you come out as against a robber, with swords and clubs to capture me? 49 Day after day I was with you in the temple teaching, and you did not seize me. But let the Scriptures be fulfilled." 50 And they all left him and fled.
51 And a young man followed him, with nothing but a linen cloth about his body. And they seized him, 52 but he left the linen cloth and ran away naked.
53 And they led Jesus to the high priest. And all the chief priests and the elders and the scribes came together. 54 And Peter had followed him at a distance, right into the courtyard of the high priest. And he was sitting with the guards and warming himself at the fire. 55 Now the chief priests and the whole council were seeking testimony

against Jesus to put him to death, but they found none. ⁵⁶ For many bore false witness against him, but their testimony did not agree. ⁵⁷ And some stood up and bore false witness against him, saying, ⁵⁸ "We heard him say, 'I will destroy this temple that is made with hands, and in three days I will build another, not made with hands.'" ⁵⁹ Yet even about this their testimony did not agree. ⁶⁰ And the high priest stood up in the midst and asked Jesus, "Have you no answer to make? What is it that these men testify against you?" ⁶¹ But he remained silent and made no answer. Again the high priest asked him, "Are you the Christ, the Son of the Blessed?" ⁶² And Jesus said, "I am, and you will see the Son of Man seated at the right hand of Power, and coming with the clouds of heaven." ⁶³ And the high priest tore his garments and said, "What further witnesses do we need? ⁶⁴ You have heard his blasphemy. What is your decision?" And they all condemned him as deserving death. ⁶⁵ And some began to spit on him and to cover his face and to strike him, saying to him, "Prophesy!" And the guards received him with blows.

➤ Scripture Reflection on Today's Reading

Put a circle around difficult words and phrases.

Put a star next to verses that cause us to praise and give thanks.

Underline verses with commands or that lead us to repent.

Put a box around key concepts and other family discussion points.

◀ Westminster Catechism Questions

Q. 91. *How do the sacraments become effectual means of salvation?*
A. The sacraments become effectual means of salvation, not from

any virtue in them, or in him that doth administer them; but only by the blessing of Christ, and the working of his Spirit in them that by faith receive them.

Q. 92. *What is a sacrament?*
A. A sacrament is an holy ordinance instituted by Christ; wherein, by sensible signs, Christ, and the benefits of the new covenant, are represented, sealed, and applied to believers.

🖐 Prayer Requests of the Week

Our Family

-
-
-
-

The Church

-
-
-
-

The World

-
-
-

🔊 The Lord's Prayer: Recite Together

Our Father which art in heaven, Hallowed be thy name. Thy kingdom come, Thy will be done in earth, as it is in heaven. Give us this day our daily bread. And forgive us our debts, as we forgive our debtors. And lead us not into temptation, but deliver us from evil: For thine is the kingdom, and the power, and the glory, forever. Amen.

🎵 Optional Singing: Select a "psalm, hymn, or spiritual song" (Ephesians 5:19), from the Psalter, the church hymnal, or a Youtube worship playlist.

➖ Exercises For Children

In the free space on this page: (1) write out one of the catechism questions, (2) practice writing out or spelling some of the key words from the Scripture reading, or (3) draw a picture of something important from today's family discussion.

Family Activity: See Appendix #1 for quality time ideas.

SERMON NOTES ON THIS WEEK'S TEXT

DATE

PREACHER

INTRODUCTION

MAIN IDEAS

PERSONAL or FAMILY APPLICATIONS

🖐 **Opening Prayer (from the Book of Common Prayer). All pray together, or head of household may lead.**

Almighty God, to whom all hearts are open, all desires known, and from whom no secrets are hid; cleanse the thoughts of our hearts by the inspiration of Thy Holy Spirit, that we may more perfectly love Thee, and more worthily magnify Thy holy name, through Jesus Christ our Lord, Amen.

📖 **Scripture Reading: Mark 14:66-72 (ESV)**

[66] And as Peter was below in the courtyard, one of the servant girls of the high priest came, [67] and seeing Peter warming himself, she looked at him and said, "You also were with the Nazarene, Jesus." [68] But he denied it, saying, "I neither know nor understand what you mean." And he went out into the gateway and the rooster crowed. [69] And the servant girl saw him and began again to say to the bystanders, "This man is one of them." [70] But again he denied it. And after a little while the bystanders again said to Peter, "Certainly you are one of them, for you are a Galilean." [71] But he began to invoke a curse on himself and to swear, "I do not know this man of whom you speak." [72] And immediately the rooster crowed a second time. And Peter remembered how Jesus had said to him, "Before the rooster crows twice, you will deny me three times." And he broke down and wept.

👉 **Scripture Reflection on Today's Reading**

Put a circle around difficult words and phrases.

Put a star next to verses that cause us to praise and give thanks.

Underline verses with commands or that lead us to repent.

Put a box around key concepts and other family discussion points.

🎓 Westminster Catechism Questions

Q. 93. *Which are the sacraments of the New Testament?*
A. The sacraments of the New Testament are baptism and the Lord's supper.

Q. 94. *What is baptism?*
A. Baptism is a sacrament, wherein the washing with water in the name of the Father, and of the Son, and of the Holy Ghost, doth signify and seal our ingrafting into Christ, and partaking of the benefits of the covenant of grace, and our engagement to be the Lord's.

🔊 Apostle's Creed: Recite as a Family

I believe in God the Father Almighty, Maker of heaven and earth. I believe in Jesus Christ, His only Son, our Lord, who was conceived by the Holy Spirit, and born of the Virgin Mary. He suffered under Pontius Pilate, was crucified, died, and was buried; he descended into hell. The third day he rose again from the dead. He ascended into heaven, he is seated at the right hand of God the Father Almighty. From there he will come to judge the living and the dead. I believe in the Holy Spirit, the holy catholic church, the communion of saints, the forgiveness of sins, the resurrection of the body, and the life everlasting. Amen.

✋ Prayer Requests of the Week

Our Family

-
-
-

The Church

-
-
-
-

The World

-
-
-

🔊 **The Lord's Prayer: Recite Together**

Our Father which art in heaven, Hallowed be thy name. Thy kingdom come, Thy will be done in earth, as it is in heaven. Give us this day our daily bread. And forgive us our debts, as we forgive our debtors. And lead us not into temptation, but deliver us from evil: For thine is the kingdom, and the power, and the glory, forever. Amen.

♪♪ **Optional Singing:** Select a "psalm, hymn, or spiritual song" (Ephesians 5:19), from the Psalter, the church hymnal, or a Youtube worship playlist.

➡ Exercises For Children

In the free space on this page: (1) write out one of the catechism questions, (2) practice writing out or spelling some of the key words from the Scripture reading, or (3) draw a picture of something important from today's family discussion.

Family Activity: See Appendix #1 for quality time ideas.

SERMON NOTES ON THIS WEEK'S TEXT

DATE

PREACHER

INTRODUCTION

MAIN IDEAS

PERSONAL or FAMILY APPLICATIONS

✋ Call to Worship, Psalm 95 KJV
(Traditionally called the Venite Exultemus Domino)

[1] O come, let us sing unto the Lord: let us make a joyful noise to the rock of our salvation. [2] Let us come before his presence with thanksgiving, and make a joyful noise unto him with psalms. [3] For the Lord is a great God, and a great King above all gods. [4] In his hand are the deep places of the earth: the strength of the hills is his also. [5] The sea is his, and he made it: and his hands formed the dry land. [6] O come, let us worship and bow down: let us kneel before the Lord our maker. [7] For he is our God; and we are the people of his pasture, and the sheep of his hand.

📖 Scripture Reading: Mark 15:1-15 (NKJV)

1 Immediately, in the morning, the chief priests held a consultation with the elders and scribes and the whole council; and they bound Jesus, led *Him* away, and delivered *Him* to Pilate. [2] Then Pilate asked Him, "Are You the King of the Jews?"
He answered and said to him, "*It is as* you say."
[3] And the chief priests accused Him of many things, but
He answered nothing. [4] Then Pilate asked Him again, saying, "Do You answer nothing? See how many things they testify against You!" [5] But Jesus still answered nothing, so that Pilate marveled.

[6] Now at the feast he was accustomed to releasing one prisoner to them, whomever they requested. [7] And there was one named Barabbas, *who was* chained with his fellow rebels; they had committed murder in the rebellion. [8] Then the multitude, crying aloud, began to ask *him to do* just as he had always done for them. [9] But Pilate answered them, saying, "Do you want me to

release to you the King of the Jews?" [10] For he knew that the chief priests had handed Him over because of envy.

[11] But the chief priests stirred up the crowd, so that he should rather release Barabbas to them. [12] Pilate answered and said to them again, "What then do you want me to do *with Him* whom you call the King of the Jews?"

[13] So they cried out again, "Crucify Him!"

[14] Then Pilate said to them, "Why, what evil has He done?" But they cried out all the more, "Crucify Him!"

[15] So Pilate, wanting to gratify the crowd, released Barabbas to them; and he delivered Jesus, after he had scourged *Him,* to be crucified.

━ Scripture Reflection on Today's Reading

Put a circle around difficult words and phrases.

Put a star next to verses that cause us to praise and give thanks.

Underline verses with commands or that lead us to repent.

Put a box around key concepts and other family discussion points.

❦ Westminster Catechism Questions

Q. 95. *To whom is baptism to be administered?*
A. Baptism is not to be administered to any that are out of the visible church, till they profess their faith in Christ, and obedience to him; but the infants of such as are members of the visible church are to be baptized.

Q. 96. *What is the Lord's supper?*
A. The Lord's supper is a sacrament, wherein, by giving and receiving bread and wine according to Christ's appointment, his

death is showed forth; and the worthy receivers are, not after a corporal and carnal manner, but by faith, made partakers of his body and blood, with all his benefits, to their spiritual nourishment and growth in grace.

🔊 Apostle's Creed: Recite as a Family

I believe in God the Father Almighty, Maker of heaven and earth. I believe in Jesus Christ, His only Son, our Lord, who was conceived by the Holy Spirit, and born of the Virgin Mary. He suffered under Pontius Pilate, was crucified, died, and was buried; he descended into hell. The third day he rose again from the dead. He ascended into heaven, he is seated at the right hand of God the Father Almighty. From there he will come to judge the living and the dead. I believe in the Holy Spirit, the holy catholic church, the communion of saints, the forgiveness of sins, the resurrection of the body, and the life everlasting. Amen.

✋ Prayer Requests of the Week

Our Family

-
-
-

The Church

-
-
-

-

-

-

🔊 The Lord's Prayer: Recite Together

Our Father which art in heaven, Hallowed be thy name. Thy kingdom come, Thy will be done in earth, as it is in heaven. Give us this day our daily bread. And forgive us our debts, as we forgive our debtors. And lead us not into temptation, but deliver us from evil: For thine is the kingdom, and the power, and the glory, forever. Amen.

🎵 Optional Singing: Select a "psalm, hymn, or spiritual song" (Ephesians 5:19), from the Psalter, the church hymnal, or a Youtube worship playlist.

▬ Exercises For Children

In the free space on this page: (1) write out one of the catechism questions, (2) practice writing out or spelling some of the key words from the Scripture reading, or (3) draw a picture of something important from today's family discussion.

SERMON NOTES ON THIS WEEK'S TEXT

DATE

PREACHER

INTRODUCTION

MAIN IDEAS

PERSONAL or FAMILY APPLICATIONS

🔥 **Opening Prayer (from the Book of Common Prayer). All pray together, or head of household may lead.**

Almighty God, to whom all hearts are open, all desires known, and from whom no secrets are hid; cleanse the thoughts of our hearts by the inspiration of Thy Holy Spirit, that we may more perfectly love Thee, and more worthily magnify Thy holy name, through Jesus Christ our Lord, Amen.

📖 **Scripture Reading: Mark 15:16-32 (NKJV)**

[16] Then the soldiers led Him away into the hall called Praetorium, and they called together the whole garrison. [17] And they clothed Him with purple; and they twisted a crown of thorns, put it on His *head,* [18] and began to salute Him, "Hail, King of the Jews!" [19] Then they struck Him on the head with a reed and spat on Him; and bowing the knee, they worshiped Him. [20] And when they had mocked Him, they took the purple off Him, put His own clothes on Him, and led Him out to crucify Him.

[21] Then they compelled a certain man, Simon a Cyrenian, the father of Alexander and Rufus, as he was coming out of the country and passing by, to bear His cross. [22] And they brought Him to the place Golgotha, which is translated, Place of a Skull. [23] Then they gave Him wine mingled with myrrh to drink, but He did not take *it.*[24] And when they crucified Him, they divided His garments, casting lots for them *to determine* what every man should take.
[25] Now it was the third hour, and they crucified Him. [26] And the inscription of His accusation was written above:
THE KING OF THE JEWS.

27 With Him they also crucified two robbers, one on His right and the other on His left. 28 So the Scripture was fulfilled which says, "And He was numbered with the transgressors."

29 And those who passed by blasphemed Him, wagging their heads and saying, "Aha! *You* who destroy the temple and build *it* in three days, 30 save Yourself, and come down from the cross!"

31 Likewise the chief priests also, mocking among themselves with the scribes, said, "He saved others; Himself He cannot save. 32 Let the Christ, the King of Israel, descend now from the cross, that we may see and believe."

Even those who were crucified with Him reviled Him.

➥ Scripture Reflection on Today's Reading

Put a circle around difficult words and phrases.

Put a star next to verses that cause us to praise and give thanks.

Underline verses with commands or that lead us to repent.

Put a box around key concepts and other family discussion points.

❦ Westminster Catechism Questions

Q. 97. *What is required to the worthy receiving of the Lord's supper?*
A. It is required of them that would worthily partake of the Lord's supper, that they examine themselves of their knowledge to discern the Lord's body, of their faith to feed upon him, of their repentance, love, and new obedience; lest, coming unworthily, they eat and drink judgment to themselves.

Q. 98. *What is prayer?*
A. Prayer is an offering up of our desires unto God, for things

agreeable to his will, in the name of Christ, with confession of our sins, and thankful acknowledgment of his mercies.

🔊 Apostle's Creed: Recite as a Family

I believe in God the Father Almighty, Maker of heaven and earth. I believe in Jesus Christ, His only Son, our Lord, who was conceived by the Holy Spirit, and born of the Virgin Mary. He suffered under Pontius Pilate, was crucified, died, and was buried; he descended into hell. The third day he rose again from the dead. He ascended into heaven, he is seated at the right hand of God the Father Almighty. From there he will come to judge the living and the dead. I believe in the Holy Spirit, the holy catholic church, the communion of saints, the forgiveness of sins, the resurrection of the body, and the life everlasting. Amen.

✋ Prayer Requests of the Week

Our Family

-
-
-

The Church

-
-
-

-

The World

-

-

-

🔊 The Lord's Prayer: Recite Together

Our Father which art in heaven, Hallowed be thy name. Thy kingdom come, Thy will be done in earth, as it is in heaven. Give us this day our daily bread. And forgive us our debts, as we forgive our debtors. And lead us not into temptation, but deliver us from evil: For thine is the kingdom, and the power, and the glory, forever. Amen.

🎶 **Optional Singing:** Select a "psalm, hymn, or spiritual song" (Ephesians 5:19), from the Psalter, the church hymnal, or a Youtube worship playlist.

➥ Exercises For Children

In the free space on this page: (1) write out one of the catechism questions, (2) practice writing out or spelling some of the key words from the Scripture reading, or (3) draw a picture of something important from today's family discussion.

Family Activity: See Appendix #1 for quality time ideas.

SERMON NOTES ON THIS WEEK'S TEXT

DATE

PREACHER

INTRODUCTION

MAIN IDEAS

PERSONAL or FAMILY APPLICATIONS

🔥 **Opening Prayer (from the Book of Common Prayer). All pray together, or head of household may lead.**

Almighty God, to whom all hearts are open, all desires known, and from whom no secrets are hid; cleanse the thoughts of our hearts by the inspiration of Thy Holy Spirit, that we may more perfectly love Thee, and more worthily magnify Thy holy name, through Jesus Christ our Lord, Amen.

📖 **Scripture Reading: Mark 15:33-41 (NKJV)**

33 Now when the sixth hour had come, there was darkness over the whole land until the ninth hour. 34 And at the ninth hour Jesus cried out with a loud voice, saying, "Eloi, Eloi, lama sabachthani?" which is translated, "My God, My God, why have You forsaken Me?" 35 Some of those who stood by, when they heard *that,* said, "Look, He is calling for Elijah!" 36 Then someone ran and filled a sponge full of sour wine, put *it* on a reed, and offered *it* to Him to drink, saying, "Let Him alone; let us see if Elijah will come to take Him down." 37 And Jesus cried out with a loud voice, and breathed His last. 38 Then the veil of the temple was torn in two from top to bottom. 39 So when the centurion, who stood opposite Him, saw that He cried out like this and breathed His last, he said, "Truly this Man was the Son of God!" 40 There were also women looking on from afar, among whom were Mary Magdalene, Mary the mother of James the Less and of Joses, and Salome, 41 who also followed Him and ministered to Him when He was in Galilee, and many other women who came up with Him to Jerusalem.

➡ **Scripture Reflection on Today's Reading**

Put a circle around difficult words and phrases.

Put a star next to verses that cause us to praise and give thanks.

Underline verses with commands or that lead us to repent.

Put a box around key concepts and other family discussion points.

🎓 Westminster Catechism Questions

Q. 99. *What rule hath God given for our direction in prayer?*
A. The whole word of God is of use to direct us in prayer; but the special rule of direction is that form of prayer which Christ taught his disciples, commonly called the Lord's prayer.

Q. 100. *What doth the preface of the Lord's prayer teach us?*
A. The preface of the Lord's prayer, which is, Our Father which art in heaven, teacheth us to draw near to God with all holy reverence and confidence, as children to a father able and ready to help us; and that we should pray with and for others.

Q. 101. *What do we pray for in the first petition?*
A. In the first petition, which is, Hallowed be thy name, we pray that God would enable us and others to glorify him in all that whereby he maketh himself known; and that he would dispose all things to his own glory.

🔊 Apostle's Creed: Recite as a Family

I believe in God the Father Almighty, Maker of heaven and earth. I believe in Jesus Christ, His only Son, our Lord, who was conceived by the Holy Spirit, and born of the Virgin Mary. He suffered under Pontius Pilate, was crucified, died, and was buried; he descended into hell. The third day he rose again from the dead. He ascended

*into heaven, he is seated at the right hand of God the Father
Almighty. From there he will come to judge the living and the dead.
I believe in the Holy Spirit, the holy catholic church, the communion
of saints, the forgiveness of sins, the resurrection of the body, and
the life everlasting. Amen.*

✋ Prayer Requests of the Week

Our Family

-

-

-

The Church

-

-

-

-

The World

-

-

-

🔊 The Lord's Prayer: Recite Together

Our Father which art in heaven, Hallowed be thy name. Thy kingdom come, Thy will be done in earth, as it is in heaven. Give us this day our daily bread. And forgive us our debts, as we forgive our debtors. And lead us not into temptation, but deliver us from evil: For thine is the kingdom, and the power, and the glory, forever. Amen.

🎵 **Optional Singing:** Select a "psalm, hymn, or spiritual song" (Ephesians 5:19), from the Psalter, the church hymnal, or a Youtube worship playlist.

➡ Exercises For Children

In the free space on this page: (1) write out one of the catechism questions, (2) practice writing out or spelling some of the key words from the Scripture reading, or (3) draw a picture of something important from today's family discussion.

Family Activity: See Appendix #1 for quality time ideas.

SERMON NOTES ON THIS WEEK'S TEXT

DATE

PREACHER

INTRODUCTION

MAIN IDEAS

PERSONAL or FAMILY APPLICATIONS

👆 Opening Prayer (from the Book of Common Prayer). All pray together, or head of household may lead.

Almighty God, to whom all hearts are open, all desires known, and from whom no secrets are hid; cleanse the thoughts of our hearts by the inspiration of Thy Holy Spirit, that we may more perfectly love Thee, and more worthily magnify Thy holy name, through Jesus Christ our Lord, Amen.

📖 Scripture Reading: Mark 15:42-47 (ESV)

[42] And when evening had come, since it was the day of Preparation, that is, the day before the Sabbath, [43] Joseph of Arimathea, a respected member of the council, who was also himself looking for the kingdom of God, took courage and went to Pilate and asked for the body of Jesus. [44] Pilate was surprised to hear that he should have already died. And summoning the centurion, he asked him whether he was already dead. [45] And when he learned from the centurion that he was dead, he granted the corpse to Joseph. [46] And Joseph bought a linen shroud, and taking him down, wrapped him in the linen shroud and laid him in a tomb that had been cut out of the rock. And he rolled a stone against the entrance of the tomb. [47] Mary Magdalene and Mary the mother of Joses saw where he was laid.

➡ Scripture Reflection on Today's Reading

Put a circle around difficult words and phrases.

Put a star next to verses that cause us to praise and give thanks.

Underline verses with commands or that lead us to repent.

Put a box around key concepts and other family discussion points.

◥ Westminster Catechism Questions

Q. 102. *What do we pray for in the second petition?*
A. In the second petition, which is, Thy kingdom come, we pray that Satan's kingdom may be destroyed; and that the kingdom of grace may be advanced, ourselves and others brought into it, and kept in it; and that the kingdom of glory may be hastened.

Q. 103. *What do we pray for in the third petition?*
A. In the third petition, which is, Thy will be done in earth, as it is in heaven, we pray that God, by his grace, would make us able and willing to know, obey and submit to his will in all things, as the angels do in heaven.

Q. 104. *What do we pray for in the fourth petition?*
A. In the fourth petition, which is, Give us this day our daily bread, we pray that of God's free gift we may receive a competent portion of the good things of this life, and enjoy his blessing with them.

◀» Apostle's Creed: Recite as a Family

I believe in God the Father Almighty, Maker of heaven and earth. I believe in Jesus Christ, His only Son, our Lord, who was conceived by the Holy Spirit, and born of the Virgin Mary. He suffered under Pontius Pilate, was crucified, died, and was buried; he descended into hell. The third day he rose again from the dead. He ascended into heaven, he is seated at the right hand of God the Father Almighty. From there he will come to judge the living and the dead. I believe in the Holy Spirit, the holy catholic church, the communion of saints, the forgiveness of sins, the resurrection of the body, and the life everlasting. Amen.

✋ Prayer Requests of the Week

Our Family

-

-

-

The Church

-

-

-

-

The World

-

-

-

🔊 The Lord's Prayer: Recite Together

Our Father which art in heaven, Hallowed be thy name. Thy kingdom come, Thy will be done in earth, as it is in heaven. Give us this day our daily bread. And forgive us our debts, as we forgive our

debtors. And lead us not into temptation, but deliver us from evil: For thine is the kingdom, and the power, and the glory, forever. Amen.

🎵 **Optional Singing:** Select a "psalm, hymn, or spiritual song" (Ephesians 5:19), from the Psalter, the church hymnal, or a Youtube worship playlist.

━ Exercises For Children
In the free space on this page: (1) write out one of the catechism questions, (2) practice writing out or spelling some of the key words from the Scripture reading, or (3) draw a picture of something important from today's family discussion.

Family Activity: See Appendix #1 for quality time ideas.

SERMON NOTES ON THIS WEEK'S TEXT

DATE

PREACHER

INTRODUCTION

MAIN IDEAS

PERSONAL or FAMILY APPLICATIONS

🔥 Call to Worship, Psalm 95 KJV
(Traditionally called the Venite Exultemus Domino)

[1] O come, let us sing unto the Lord: let us make a joyful noise to the rock of our salvation. [2] Let us come before his presence with thanksgiving, and make a joyful noise unto him with psalms. [3] For the Lord is a great God, and a great King above all gods. [4] In his hand are the deep places of the earth: the strength of the hills is his also. [5] The sea is his, and he made it: and his hands formed the dry land. [6] O come, let us worship and bow down: let us kneel before the Lord our maker. [7] For he is our God; and we are the people of his pasture, and the sheep of his hand.

▉ Scripture Reading: Mark 16:1-20 (ESV)

When the Sabbath was past, Mary Magdalene, Mary the mother of James, and Salome bought spices, so that they might go and anoint him. [2] And very early on the first day of the week, when the sun had risen, they went to the tomb. [3] And they were saying to one another, "Who will roll away the stone for us from the entrance of the tomb?" [4] And looking up, they saw that the stone had been rolled back—it was very large. [5] And entering the tomb, they saw a young man sitting on the right side, dressed in a white robe, and they were alarmed. [6] And he said to them, "Do not be alarmed. You seek Jesus of Nazareth, who was crucified. He has risen; he is not here. See the place where they laid him. [7] But go, tell his disciples and Peter that he is going before you to Galilee. There you will see him, just as he told you." [8] And they went out and fled from the tomb, for trembling and astonishment had seized them, and they said nothing to anyone, for they were afraid.

[Some of the earliest manuscripts do not include 16:9–20.]

[9] Now when he rose early on the first day of the week, he appeared first to Mary Magdalene, from whom he had cast out seven demons. [10] She went and told those who had been with him, as they mourned and wept. [11] But when they heard that he was alive and had been seen by her, they would not believe it.

[12] After these things he appeared in another form to two of them, as they were walking into the country. [13] And they went back and told the rest, but they did not believe them.

[14] Afterward he appeared to the eleven themselves as they were reclining at table, and he rebuked them for their unbelief and hardness of heart, because they had not believed those who saw him after he had risen. [15] And he said to them, "Go into all the world and proclaim the gospel to the whole creation. [16] Whoever believes and is baptized will be saved, but whoever does not believe will be condemned. [17] And these signs will accompany those who believe: in my name they will cast out demons; they will speak in new tongues; [18] they will pick up serpents with their hands; and if they drink any deadly poison, it will not hurt them; they will lay their hands on the sick, and they will recover."

[19] So then the Lord Jesus, after he had spoken to them, was taken up into heaven and sat down at the right hand of God. [20] And they went out and preached everywhere, while the Lord worked with them and confirmed the message by accompanying signs.

⚊ Scripture Reflection on Today's Reading

Put a circle around difficult words and phrases.

Put a star next to verses that cause us to praise and give thanks.

Underline verses with commands or that lead us to repent.

Put a box around key concepts and other family discussion points.

🎓 Westminster Catechism Questions

Q. 105. *What do we pray for in the fifth petition?*
A. In the fifth petition, which is, And forgive us our debts, as we forgive our debtors, we pray that God, for Christ's sake, would freely pardon all our sins; which we are the rather encouraged to ask, because by his grace we are enabled from the heart to forgive others.

Q. 106. *What do we pray for in the sixth petition?*
A. In the sixth petition, which is, And lead us not into temptation, but deliver us from evil, we pray that God would either keep us from being tempted to sin, or support and deliver us when we are tempted.

Q. 107. *What doth the conclusion of the Lord's prayer teach us?*
A. The conclusion of the Lord's prayer, which is, For thine is the kingdom, and the power, and the glory, forever, Amen, teacheth us to take our encouragement in prayer from God only, and in our prayers to praise him, ascribing kingdom, power and glory to him. And in testimony of our desire, and assurance to be heard, we say, Amen.

🔊 Apostle's Creed: Recite as a Family

I believe in God the Father Almighty, Maker of heaven and earth. I believe in Jesus Christ, His only Son, our Lord, who was conceived by the Holy Spirit, and born of the Virgin Mary. He suffered under Pontius Pilate, was crucified, died, and was buried; he descended into hell. The third day he rose again from the dead. He ascended into heaven, he is seated at the right hand of God the Father Almighty. From there he will come to judge the living and the dead. I believe in the Holy Spirit, the holy catholic church, the communion of saints, the forgiveness of sins, the resurrection of the body, and the life everlasting. Amen.

✋ Prayer Requests of the Week

Our Family

-

-

-

The Church

-

-

-

-

The World

-

-

-

🔊 The Lord's Prayer: Recite Together

Our Father which art in heaven, Hallowed be thy name. Thy kingdom come, Thy will be done in earth, as it is in heaven. Give us this day our daily bread. And forgive us our debts, as we forgive our debtors. And lead us not into temptation, but deliver us from evil: For thine is the kingdom, and the power, and the glory, forever. Amen.

🎵 Optional Singing: Select a "psalm, hymn, or spiritual song" (Ephesians 5:19), from the Psalter, the church hymnal, or a Youtube worship playlist.

▬ Exercises For Children

In the free space on this page: (1) write out one of the catechism questions, (2) practice writing out or spelling some of the key words from the Scripture reading, or (3) draw a picture of something important from today's family discussion.

Family Activity: See Appendix #1 for quality time ideas.

SERMON NOTES ON THIS WEEK'S TEXT

DATE

PREACHER

INTRODUCTION

MAIN IDEAS

PERSONAL or FAMILY APPLICATIONS

Appendix One: Family Activity Ideas. Check off each activity as your family enjoys them. Feel free to use these ideas in any order that you choose.

- ☐ Walk around the block or property
- ☐ Collect leaves in the neighborhood and discuss
- ☐ Write a "Thank You" letter to someone who cares about you
- ☐ Make a meal for a neighbor
- ☐ Look over family photos
- ☐ Create a simple family tree craft
- ☐ Rock painting
- ☐ Read aloud short stories
- ☐ Tell the birth or adoption story of each person in the family
- ☐ Treasure hunt
- ☐ Geocaching (Google it)
- ☐ Plant something – tree, bush, flowers
- ☐ Make a card for a widow or shut-in from your church
- ☐ Write a letter to a soldier serving our armed forces
- ☐ Make a meal for a widow

- ☐ Charades
- ☐ Spoons (card game)
- ☐ Hiking in the neighborhood park
- ☐ Feed the squirrels
- ☐ Star gazing and identification. A simple book or app may help
- ☐ Bike ride
- ☐ Lawn games – bocce ball, corn hole etc.
- ☐ Serve volunteer
- ☐ Fly a kite
- ☐ Make a traditional picnic lunch
- ☐ Bonfire and stories
- ☐ Hide the penny game in the house
- ☐ Frisbee in the yard
- ☐ Bake cookies for a neighbor you have not seen in a while

Appendix Two: Sources

The Holy Bible. Scripture quotations marked ESV are from *The Holy Bible, English Standard Version.* Copyright © 2017, by Crossway Bibles, a Division of Good News Publishers. All rights reserved.

Scripture quotations marked NKJV are from the New King James Version®. Copyright © 1982 by Thomas Nelson. Used by permission. All rights reserved.

Scripture quotations marked KJV are from the King James Version (Authorized Version) of the Bible. Public Domain.

The Ten Commandments and the Lord's Prayer are cited from the King James Version (Authorized Version) of the Bible to retain the traditional language.

The Book of Common Prayer of 1662. (Cambridge University Press. UK).

The Trinity Hymnal (Atlanta, GA: Great Commission Publications), 1994.

The Psalms of David in Meter: 1650 Church of Scotland Edition (London, UK: Trinitarian Bible Society), 2018.

The Westminster Shorter Catechism, (Lawrenceville, GA: The Christian Education and Publication Committee, Presbyterian Church in America), 2007.

Made in the USA
Middletown, DE
22 January 2022

59416505R00159